Snapshots...

Growing up Behind the Iron Curtain

Eva M. Kende

Written by:
Eva M. Kende B.Sc.

Published by:
Try Kay Enterprises
P.O. Box 8084
Canmore, AB.
T1W 2T8
Canada
www.telusplanet.net/public/ekende
Phone/fax: 403-678-5821

Cover photo:
Zumo taking a snapshot
through a mirror with Eva in his arm

ISBN 0-9691659-2-7
Printed in Canada by:
Blitzprint Inc.

Dedicated to my grandsons,
Noah and Anthony,
so that in time they may understand...

Table of Contents

Snapshots –Introduction

As I age, I become more introspective. I'm not "living in the past," but I dip into my memories to understand the present; how I journeyed through this life and what made me the person I am. My memory is like the photos in our family album. The years during and immediately after the war are particularly hazy, like faded daguerreotypes; but, at times, this introspection has illuminated minute incidents, as a flashbulb does when taking a snapshot. Each detail, including taste and smell, becomes suddenly clear and pure. I strung such snapshots together to create this book. It is autobiographical, but because they live in my memory as unconnected stories, I chose not to dilute the vividness of these vignettes with invention, or the embroidering of vague recollections. Therefore, I opted for the form of short essays or fireside tales to deal with specific topics. The format makes chronological organization difficult and some repetition is unavoidable, but it better reflects how a snapshot of memory brings into focus a series of events.

The parts that refer to periods before my birth I gleaned mostly from my grandmother's tales. At first, I planned to rely solely on my own memories, but it became clear that they were hollow without a background, so I used her oft-told tales to weave a backdrop.

Many authors have written books about communism, the politics of it, the cruel imprisonments, the Hungarian revolution and the mysterious Iron Curtain. However, few of those works said much about the everyday lives of ordinary people, especially children. The period I cover is post-war until the Hungarian Revolution and our resulting flight to Canada. For interest's sake, I have added some notes in italics at the end of some of the stories to explain how things tie into the present. Mostly, I used the real first names of the participants in my stories; only in a few instances did I change the names, where I felt that using their real names might compromise their privacy.

I didn't write these stories to elicit horror or pity. As I got older and friends plied me with questions about my experiences, I realized that what I lived through wasn't a normal state of events, but a rather ugly piece of history.

For those who are interested, I added a short Historical Background and a List of Internet Sites in English in the Appendix.

"Snapshots" is my personal celebration of the 50th anniversary of the Hungarian Revolution of 1956.

Eva on her Körút, 1943

Background

Rózsi

Whenever my mother really wanted to hurt me, she would declare, "You're just like your grandmother!" Little did she know my secret: I loved and admired my grandmother. Oh, I was aware of her many faults — her unbridled snobbery, her self-absorption and her haughtiness, but she had a zest for life that even today, more than forty years after her death, sends tingles of excitement through my soul.

Rózsi, my grandmother, was born in 1878, the only daughter of a poor family with three boys. Life must have been a struggle, because she quit school after grade six to work and help put the two younger brothers through school. No wonder she was extraordinarily proud of her brothers, who became well-known architects and wealthy men. A young woman at that time usually didn't get much education because parents presumed that they'd marry and become the husband's responsibility. Like many other girls, she went into apprenticeship to learn a trade. She became a necktie maker. At the end of the nineteenth century and into the twentieth, gentlemen wouldn't appear in public without a stiff collar and a tie. Many styles were fashionable among the elite, each tie announcing the social status and taste preference of its wearer. Her nimble fingers created just the right tie for each customer. During her free time, she read everything she could lay her hands on, even books that "nice" girls weren't supposed to read. When Emile Zola's forbidden Nana was discovered under her pillow, her father's rage at her for reading such books sent tremors through the family. Rózsi, however, paid little heed. She just hid her books better.

Her exploits kept her father shaking his head. He never knew what this daughter of his would get into next. The three boys were conservative and all had good positions, but Rózsi worried him. At seventeen, when she should have been looking for a husband, she announced she was going to open a shop to sell collars, shirts and her handmade ties. She held onto her dream and when she completed her apprenticeship, she put her plans into action. Since a woman in those days could neither get a permit to open a shop, nor sign a lease for such, she coerced her eldest brother, a staid bookkeeper with a large seed firm, to front for her. The year was 1901 and she was twenty-three years old. All the paperwork went under her brother's name, but she was the boss. She was an inch shy of five feet, and had hands the size of an eight-year-old. You wouldn't think she could carry off being a boss, but she did. Her erect bearing, defiant chin and elegant dress made up for her lack of height. She always dressed in the height of fashion, carefully choosing the right hat, gloves, and other accessories to complete her look. She never left home looking less than perfect.

Her shop was located in a lean-to that housed two or three similar shops on the corner side of Servita Church, across from City Hall and a block from the central Post Office, near Váci Street, the heart of the upper crust fashion district of Budapest. She did her custom and repair work in the loft whose ceiling would have been too low for anyone else. The shop, beautifully furnished in dark rosewood, with built-in cabinets to store her stock, was her pride and joy. A shiny chrome-trimmed stove stood in the corner with six tubular indentations to maximize its heat output. Near Christmas, Rózsi bought a few broken spruce branches and put them into the holes. The heated needles filled the little store with their perfume, creating a festive atmosphere. The counter had a glass panel where she displayed her samples. She sat, or rather held court, on a small dais in a bentwood Tonette chair guarding the till in the back corner while her helper, cousin Frida, sat near the window at the opposite end, bent over some fine hand stitching that was the finishing touch on a new cravat, or repairing someone's old favourite.

While she was a talented tie maker, she was even more talented in understanding human nature. Dealing with people and sympathizing at the right moment was her forte. She was the darling of the bureaucrats of City Hall, because she would lovingly restore their favourite ties and listen attentively to any woes they might have had.

She had a ball establishing her postage-stamp-size store and building her clientele. Meanwhile, her parents watched in distress as she turned down one promising suitor after another. She was almost considered an old maid when, at thirty, she finally married my grandfather, the tall, handsome Vilmos whose military bearing was a perfect foil for her diminutive, rotund proportions.

To the horror of all concerned, but reluctantly accepted by her husband, she continued running her shop after her marriage. Exactly nine months after their wedding, she gave birth to a healthy boy, Róbert, and less than a year later to a pretty girl, my mother, Iréne. Vilmos was earning a good living and climbing the corporate ladder rapidly in a very large firm that manufactured everything from canned goods to sewing machines and many items for the war effort, including ammunition.

At first, Rózsi hired a cook-housekeeper and a nursemaid for the children, and as they grew, she replaced the nursemaid with a schwester, a German nanny, who spoke no Hungarian, so her offspring could become bilingual. It was the last days of the Austro-Hungarian monarchy where speaking fluent German was essential to everyday life. Rózsi was pleased when her beloved mother, Mária, widowed by then, came to live in her home. Mária was happy with her life, too. She had the comforts of a modern home with staff to do the hard work, but she was needed to oversee their activities. She had leisure time for her knitting, crocheting or pulling apart bits of silk remnants from Rózsi's store, while the children played at her feet. She worked on the silk remnants as a recycling project, for she could bear no waste after the many lean years of her early life. When a big sack full of silk was plucked to threads, they shipped it to Czechoslovakia to be made into a blanket. She was in her seventies, and often nodded off while working on the silk bits, her head dipping toward the sack. Iréne and Róbert crept up and blew into the lint, which rose and tickled their grandmother's nose, waking her from the unscheduled nap. The children laughed and Mária pretended to be angry with them, but not for long. All Iréne had to do was to snuggle up to her and look at her with those big brown eyes and all was forgiven.

Rózsi's brothers visited frequently with their children. The house rang with the cousins' chatter, giggles and laughter. Mária had six grandchildren and loved them all, but little Iréne, the only girl, was her favourite. Her daughter often admonished her for spoiling the child, but Iréne could charm her into just about anything, including forbidden sweets before dinner. Róbert, taking his cue from Mária, further spoiled his little sister. From an early age, he protected her from harm. The two of them, Iréne and Róbert, were co-conspirators in every mischief that, usually, Iréne instigated. One of their infamous high jinks happened when they were about six and seven, an important foreign visitor came to their home and, naturally, Rózsi wanted to show off her lovely children. But they hid under the dining room table, which was covered with a floor-length cloth. No amount of coaxing, threats or force could get them out of their hiding place until the visitor left. To hear Iréne retell this story, it was an act of rebellion.

Together they disobeyed the nanny, cajoled treats out of the cook, and played pranks on their father. Vilmos could create games and toys from a bit of string and bits of wood or matches that he had in his pocket. His creative genius reached its apex when Róbert was recovering from scarlet fever. He was well, but not yet allowed to leave home. Children with communicable diseases were quarantined for a specified length of time by order of the official physician of public health. To keep the bored child happy, Vilmos built a house from rolled-up newspapers in the middle of the room, big enough for Robert to sit in.

On Sundays, Rózsi dressed the children and herself in the finest duds and with Vilmos in tow, she went to the promenade on the bank of the Danube River to show off her family. Her customers, judges, city officials and literary notables commented on her lovely children, while her envious friends watched. Sated, she returned home to get ready for her workweek.

As the First World War cast its shadow over Budapest and

the rest of the world, my grandmother, Rózsi, seemed to have achieved all she wanted. She had a thriving business with her maiden name emblazoned on the portal, and on the finely-crafted goods she sold. The whole city knew that Nasch neckties were the very best, and that the upper crust rubbed shoulders in her shop.

The horrors of the war barely touched Budapest. The battles were fought in faraway fields, and one could always look the other way when a sick or crippled soldier passed on the street. The brief republic, the ensuing communist revolution and the white terror that followed were an annoying interlude, but didn't interfere with the comfortable middle class existence Rózsi had built. The only tale I heard from that period was that Iréne, about nine years old at the time, was petrified of the hordes of Romanian soldiers, their open campfires and snorting horses encamped on the square near their home, in front of her school, which lasted for several weeks. This brief event left an indelible fear of all things military on my mother.

The prosperous period that followed overshadowed the unpleasantness of the war years. Rózsi's business boomed and she was a celebrated craftswoman extraordinaire. She won many competitions for her beautiful work, her designs, her window displays and as a contributor to the Hungarian display at the Paris Exposition. The family spent a month every summer in a rented cottage in the hills near Budapest, and travelled occasionally to present-day Slovakia and Croatia to medicinal baths for Rózsi's arthritis. She always came back with fresh ideas and new materials for her ties.

Rózsi lavished everything she never had in her youth on her children, partly out of parental love, but also to show the world that she'd arrived. The best private schools, piano lessons, dancing, tennis, figure skating, English lessons for Róbert and conversational French for Iréne were part of their upbringing. They rubbed shoulders with the rich in their private schools and in their social activities. As they reached their teens, life was a whirlwind of parties, masquerades, dances, formal balls, tennis games and ice dancing. Iréne's humour, ease of light conversation and good looks made her very popular in social circles. Brother and sister went to all the activities together. He looked out for his little sister, and Iréne basked in the attentions of Róbert's friends.

When Róbert graduated from high school, Vilmos wanted him to join the firm where he worked. He even took him to the factory to show him the fascinating modern equipment that automated all facets of manufacturing household goods, now that peace reigned. Although Róbert showed his appreciation for what he saw and his father's passion, he wasn't interested. Róbert's heart was set on becoming an architect. Harsh arguments ensued in the family, with loyal little sister standing up for her brother. Rózsi too supported her son, flattered by his wish to emulate two of her brothers who were architects. Géza, the younger of the two uncles, mentored Róbert. He gave Róbert a job as assistant in his firm, then encouraged him to go to Vienna to study architecture. After graduating, Róbert returned to work for a number of other important architects. The rift between father and son, due to Robert's career decision, never mended, affecting Iréne's relationship with her father forever.

Even as she aged, Rózsi never lost her spunk. Trade was slow after the Second World War, but she and Frida bravely carried on. My earliest recollection of them in the shop was in 1946, when they valiantly cleared out the rubble, the broken windows and fallen plaster left by the battle of Budapest, retrieved some of their stock from the Servita monks who had safeguarded it, and resumed their positions in the shop. They wore black dresses for business with a large lace-edged jabot at the neck. They were both close to 70 seventy years old by then. Because of their attire, my mother jokingly called them the two penguins.

They reminisced about the fine gentlemen who in the pre-war years brought their own silk from Paris, or other exotic places they'd visited, to have them make their ties just the way they liked it. Rózsi had a big book with the likes, dislikes and width preferences of her clients, just to make sure she had it right. She often talked to me about the many artisans' displays and window decorating competitions she won through the years, pointing to her gold and silver medals displayed in a glass showcase.

In 1947 at age sixty-nine, she declared that she had to fly at least once before she died. We were vacationing in a village near Debrecen. A commercial flight went to Debrecen from Budapest once or twice a week, and she was going to take that to pay us a visit. This was declared in such a fashion that no one dared to bring up any objection, but the family smirked behind her back, because local planes were very rudimentary in those days and she would have been much more comfortable taking the train. I remember leaving the village in a horse-drawn cart to go to the Debrecen airport to greet my grandmother. It was a very hot July day. There wasn't a tree in sight on the limitless flat plain. The airport was little more than a rocky cow pasture, and the scheduled commercial flight was no more than a six-seater single engine propeller plane. It stopped a long way from us. The steps were lowered, and grandmother alit with perfect composure wearing a hat, crocheted lace gloves and a brown foulard silk suit with a pleated skirt. A gusty wind was blowing, so with one hand she held her hat in place while with the other she secured the folds of her voluminous skirt to keep it from blowing up into her face. She was a picture of elegance and poise in an incongruous setting as she waddled across the rocky field on two-inch heels to where we waited. She was very pleased with herself and her trip so far, but when she saw the peasant wagon in which she was to travel to the village, her eyes opened wide and her eyebrows shot up to her hairline. Since she had no choice, however, she climbed aboard while my stepfather helped by pushing her rump from below. With difficulty, she tried to compose herself, but when the carriage entered the wide avenue of Lombard poplars, she was so impressed with the grandeur of the tree-lined road that she forgot to complain. It was a fitting prelude to my stepfather's grand estate house.

Scurrying staff of all sorts had been instructed to make her comfortable. Her room was spacious and shaded from the hot prairie sun by overhanging eaves. The front yard was a lush green lawn, sheltered by untrimmed hedges from the main highway traffic that ran beside it. There was a heavy table in the centre under the old walnut tree where Rózsi and I had our meals. For breakfast, we had fresh bread with home-churned butter and cheese. I had hot chocolate, while Rózsi sipped her espresso. Lunch was the cooked main meal and we were joined by my stepfather, Zoli and my mother to have fried chicken, pork gulash or a hearty soup with handmade sweet pasta for dessert. Dinner was eggs, cold cuts or cheese with more fresh bread and homemade pickles. All the ingredients of the meals were the fresh products of the farm. Not once did Rózsi venture to the back courtyard where the pigsty, chicken coops and stables were. She never saw the staid mulberry tree nor the vast expanse of golden wheat fields beyond that, where red poppies and blue bachelor buttons bloomed on the edge of the crop, but she had a great time playing the dowager, being waited on by many servants and her attentive son-in-law in this old-fashioned setting.

She had the same hauteur in everything she did. We never saw her carrying a parcel, declaring that ladies don't carry packages. Since delicacies were so rare, she couldn't afford to miss the opportunity to buy them when she saw them. In winter, she wore a black seal coat with enormous pockets. When she got home, all manner of cold cuts and other goodies emerged from their depths. I imagine she could hide the contents of a well-filled grocery bag in those pockets. In summer, she was limited to the size of her spacious purse. Grandmother and I loved Pálpusztai, a cheese whose odour reminds one of unwashed socks. Whenever she found some, she had to buy it for the two of us to share. This was before packaging reached Europe from the USA; the cheese came wrapped in a slip of tissue paper.

Except for a very brief period in the late forties, Rózsi lived with us and shared my bedroom. We were pals. She knitted and crocheted dresses for my dolls, talked about the past, created a masterpiece needlepoint carpet for my dollhouse and read books to me. I think she actually liked my stepfather Zoli, the bumbling country squire who lacked the sophistication and social graces that Rózsi and my mother valued so much. He told her at length about his dreams to make his estate more profitable, plying her with such foreign notions —to her— as switching from the fat Hungarian pigs to the leaner English varieties, using the waste bran of his flour mill to feed the pigs, and starting a small commercial still to produce pálinka, a kind of brandy, from fallen, overripe fruit.

She sympathized when the farm was nationalized in 1949, and like a fish out of water, Zoli trudged to work as a lowly bookkeeper at the Közért grocery distribution center. All those dreams of modernized farming evaporated overnight. He didn't complain, but we sensed his disappointment. He wasn't alone. Daily news of friends losing their farms, businesses, their life's efforts, reached us in such a number that no one could focus on just one tragedy. But throughout it all, the little necktie shop stood its ground, like an invincible island in a stormy sea. Rózsi, with her usual confidence and optimism, declared: "We won't be nationalized until the sixtieth minute of the hour! We're too small."

The "sixtieth minute" came in 1953; the axe fell on a glorious summer morning. Government men entered Rózsi's shop and told her it was all over. Rózsi and Frida had to leave immediately as they sealed up the shop. They could take nothing with them, not even her awards. Rózsi was crushed, but she wasn't down long. She mourned for a week, then put on her best hat and claimed the offered job at a tie restoration cooperative. She was seventy-five. In the cramped workshop, she toiled under a naked bulb for eight hours a day and competed with the younger coworkers in speed and quality of work. Restoration meant taking the tie apart, washing it in a basin of gasoline, removing the frayed part, ironing it, inserting a new lining with stiffening, then re-stitching it carefully by hand. Eventually, age and a heart condition caught up with her and she retired, without medical insurance or a pension, since the self-employed had no such rights. For a short while, she continued to do tie restoration in our apartment, but lean times and her age forced her to give it up.

My mother decided Rózsi could earn her keep by helping with meal preparation, so that she could work longer hours. By that time, my mother and stepfather were divorced, and my mother had to provide for all three of us.

No bigger disaster could have happened than to put this businesswoman into a kitchen. Even she wouldn't eat her own cooking. If we were to be saved from starvation, I had to roll up my sleeves and learn. So I learned from cookbooks and from neighbours, putting to good use the techniques observed sitting in the kitchen and chatting with the maids in more affluent times. Grandmother gave high praise to my efforts. I don't know if the approval was really for the taste of the food I prepared or in celebration of the fact that she didn't have to do it, but she ate with gusto everything I made. During the cleaning up and dishwashing, I had my conversational German lessons from her.

Rózsi was brought up in a bilingual family, and her Austrian German was impeccable. Before the communist takeover, everyone took German as a second language in school. Then, suddenly, Russian replaced it, but most children whose parents could afford it took private German or English lessons. I had some private lessons, but as money was short, I had to stop. Grandmother took on the job. We washed dishes, dusted, polished brass and went for long walks "in German." Speaking Hungarian was forbidden at these times.

As I got older, we read books together and discussed them while taking a walk in the park. She didn't believe in censorship, so she let me loose, to my mother's horror, in my uncle's abandoned library. She said, "If she can understand it, she's ready for it! If she can't, I won't explain." I remember one of those books she wouldn't explain. Now I know it was a novel about lesbians, but at the time I read the book from cover to cover without getting anything out of it. I read it only to show I could. She approved of my choices when it came to the French classics, Prosper Mérimée, Dumas, Maupassant and Balzac, and we held long discussions about some of the finer details of these books. My mother just shook her head. She thought reading books was a waste of time.

Rózsi's thirst for knowledge never waned. She read copiously and when she read all the books available in our home and that of our friends and neighbours, she sent me to the neighbourhood branch library with a list. It was a musty, dingy place where I had to find the right call number in the card catalogue and present my order to the stern librarian at the desk. Bit by bit, as I became familiar with the system, my fear of these trips abated and my life-long love of libraries began.

We were inseparable cohorts, particularly during the summer months when school was out. She dedicated her time totally to me, except for the two hours in the late afternoon when she held court with her friends at her usual corner table at Szalay's, the outdoor café a few blocks from our apartment. She prepared for these outings with meticulous care. Freshly starched and ironed jabot decorated her carefully mended, threadbare dress. A rakish hat and crocheted lace gloves were a must.

In the meantime, huge fights I couldn't understand broke out, usually while I was out of the apartment, between my mother and my grandmother. I got a garbled version from each of them when I got home. I gathered most of their rows centered on money. One of the arguments arose about Rózsi spending money on a new haircut and a perm. The Maximka style —you would call it Afro now— copied from a film hero's hairstyle was all the rage in Budapest. At that time, Mother was practicing, economy by wearing her hair in a bun and skipping her permanent. It irked her to see her mother sporting the latest style while she, the younger eligible woman, looked frumpy. Accusations flew back and forth, each demanding my loyalties. I adored my mother and felt very protective of her, recognizing her inability to cope with the realities of the harsh life she was dealt, but Rózsi was my special buddy, my friend and confidant.

Eventually, the inevitable happened. Mother found an old folks home on the outskirts of the city and Rózsi moved there. In the strange surroundings, our intimacy was broken, but I still enjoyed her company. The fights between Rózsi and my mother continued and at one point, I was forbidden to visit my grandmother. But I was a big girl by then, fourteen years old, and while mother worked, I took the streetcar ride, a half-an-hour each way, at least once a week to visit my grandmother behind my mother's back.

Then the revolution happened and we left Hungary, without Rózsi. To ease my conscience, I left strict instructions that my grandmother should have my stylish new winter coat —I was wearing my mother's fur trimmed one while she had her lambskin coat for the trip across the border— and my most prized possession: the new crepe-soled shoes. That was all I could think of to do to please her.

She died about two years later, cared for by Luli, her nephew, and his wife Erzsike, using the proceeds of the sale of our apartment to keep her in style. She's gone, but her feisty sprit is alive still today in the depths of my soul.

———

Today, when I'm in Hungary and I open a little square of Pálpusztai, now carefully packed in foil to reduce its offensiveness, I always think of my grandmother. I can almost smell her fur coat with the foul odour of Pálpusztai, permanently embedded in the silk lining, emanating from it.

Amazingly, in 1990, Róbert, suffering so severely from advanced Alzheimer's disease that he could hardly function anymore, remembered the newspaper house when I reminded him of it. He could no longer express him self in speech, but answered me by playing the trick his father used to do with his hands. I understood.

Family Lore and Memories

My Uncle Róbert's tuition and expenses at the Technische Hochschule in Vienna were costly, and the worldwide recession was beginning to reach Hungary, too. My grandmother Rózsi's debts were piling up. In fact, only an emergency loan from one of her brothers kept her out of bankruptcy. The harsh reality was lost on my mother Iréne, now in her early twenties. She missed her brother, her constant companion, and couldn't understand why they had to move into a less elegant apartment, give up some of the servants, and to skimp on everything. The diminished circumstances were especially hard on her, because a girl of her social standing was expected to have a substantial dowry if she were to marry well. One by one, the suitors evaporated as the family's means were reduced. Brooding in the dingy apartment, Iréne blamed her mother's bad money management for her misfortune. She worked in the store and spent the rest of her time volunteering in charitable societies. As her friends married one by one, Iréne became increasingly bitter and worried. With Róbert away at school, she had no one to give her guidance or solace. Finally, through a friend, she was introduced to a wealthy man who wasn't interested in a dowry.

That man was my father, affectionately called Zumo by his family and friends. He came from a very poor family of four boys and one girl. His father died when he was sixteen and since his two older brothers were conscripts in the army fighting WWI, he had to, with a heavy heart, quit school and go to work to support his mother and the two much younger siblings. He worked hard until his older brothers returned to keep the little family afloat. Eventually, Zumo and his older brother Gyula started an auto parts business, at first in the spare room with his mother and younger siblings helping to assemble the imported bits, such as mirrors and their frames, into sellable parts. By the time he met Iréne, they had a thriving wholesale business in the fast-growing automobile trade. Iréne's elegance, good looks, dark hair and eyes, as well as her light-hearted banter and sense of humour smote him. He had struggled to take care of his mother and siblings for many years, and was now ready to have a family and home of his own. He adored his wife, although he often chided her for her extravagance in clothes and especially hats. Their home was opulent, with custom-made furniture designed by Róbert and made from Rózsi's black oak old-fashioned dining room suite. Rózsi and Vilmos gave up their home and moved to a "pension" —a small residential hotel— where a large staff catered to them.

Zumo loved to add art pieces to the décor of his home and haunted the auction houses for paintings, china and jewellery to lavish on his wife. They traveled every year to Italy, the French Riviera or Switzerland, taking many pictures on the way. Iréne was happy, but for one thing. All of her friends were having children, except her. Increasingly, she looked at young mothers with envy. The war had begun in Poland already, but she held to her plan of having a child of her own with determination. Poland and Germany seemed too far away to affect her life. Although her father Vilmos warned all who would listen about the dire consequences when Hitler came to power in 1933, Iréne wrote him off as an old pessimist. I arrived in the fall of 1941, to the delight of both families, and immediately won my father's heart. He was totally smitten by me, and dedicated his every spare minute to taking care of me or talking about me.

Iréne loved all the attention, the luxury baby carriage, the cute outfits and showing off her child. Visitors came to admire me, her husband was attentive and brought her flowers. She was the center of attention and she didn't have to deny herself anything. It never occurred to her that the future was bleak. In fact, when Vilmos again voiced his fears of the future, she waved her hand and said: "Come on, Daddy, you're always seeing things so black."

It was only when Zumo was called up and the bombs

started to fall that she grasped she was alone and had to cope. That was when she realized a child was a responsibility and not just a doll to dress and groom. The war petrified her. The uncertainty, falling bombs, lack of food and lack of opportunity for her fastidious personal hygiene were almost more than she could bear.

The last days were particularly bad. Although the Russians had liberated Pest, the Germans were shelling day and night from Margit Island just across the river from Uncle Géza's apartment where the family stayed. When the battle was over, she went to see her home, stepping over carcasses of people and horses buried under the unusually heavy snowfall that Budapest experienced that winter. She found her apartment in ruins, her lovely furniture under the rubble. Her heart stopped when she looked out to the balcony. The storage cabinet was open and the bottle of liqueur that she and Zumo were to open in celebration when he returned was lying in front of it, broken. She sensed that he was gone forever. Her worst fear was confirmed a few months later.

My earliest memories —if you can call them that— begin somewhere near my third birthday with recollections too vague to even describe. My father is very hard to capture. It's hard to know where memory leaves off and frequently repeated family tales begin. I was barely three years old when I saw my father for the last time. I was often told by my mother that he loved to put me to bed at night; he would spend a long time talking to me, then would sing me to sleep with folk songs and army marching songs, which he learned in his conscript days. In later years, my mother would mention his choices of music with disdain, obviously disapproving of his selections. Given her education in classical music, these songs weren't refined enough for her taste. I didn't argue with her. Songs like these were never played in our home during my childhood, yet I love them passionately. When we had maids, I begged them to sing me to sleep with folk songs. Mother shook her head, but didn't really object. Through these songs, I felt able to touch that pure, uncompromising love my father gave me when he stood by my crib on his last days at home. I can only suspect that the music stirs up the faint memory of him singing these songs to me. I have no picture in my mind, but the music stirs my emotions in a powerful way. I have a large collection of tapes and records. Even today, when I'm in need of emotional comfort, I can draw solace from the folk songs, but the effect of the marching songs is more profound. I never heard the war marches until I was in my thirties, because most of them were banned by the communist regime as a reminder of the old system of government. That's when I got hold of a beat-up old record. The effect was unbelievable. I bought several newer tapes since the ban on this type of music was lifted in Hungary about fifteen years ago. Even today, they grab me by the heart and squeeze my emotions until I find tears rolling down my cheeks. When the tape or record is over, I feel drained, but much better.

What he talked to me about, I have no idea. Growing up, I imagined him sharing with me his values, and his fears of not being there for me; above all, I think he talked about the responsibility I had to look after my mother. I sensed this rather than knew, but remember standing up for my mother, at a very early age, fiercely defending her or giving her support as an adult would. Thirty years later, when my Uncle Róbert — my mother's brother — died and my aunt sent me my father's letters, I saw that I was right. As I read the letters from my father written to Róbert, my suspicions were confirmed. He described in detail his foreboding about the looming war and his concerns for the welfare of his family. The words and expressions sounded very familiar.

I only get certain glimpses of the months of the battle of Budapest, about events that must have been very important to me.

I clearly remember my thirteen year old cousin Tomi on his knees, tying the feet of two armchairs facing each other together to make a bed for me. I can see his tousled blond curls as he bent his head in concentration over the task. I sense, rather than remember, his soothing words, and the comfort I drew from them amidst frightening noises of battle outside. We, eight of us, were living with Uncle Géza and his wife in their apartment during the final weeks of the war. With not enough beds to accommodate so many people, the two upholstered armchairs, tied together, became my bed every night.

Another picture I see is my Great-Uncle Géza and Great-Aunt Aranka sitting in bed among fluffy white pillows like a Rembrandt painting, Géza, still handsome with his dark hair and full beard, next to Aranka, her bush of frizzy blonde hair surrounding her round face. Every night, they invited me into their bedroom. Then I heard a knock from the general direction of the bed, and I was to look for my nightly treat: a little square of chocolate was hidden somewhere in the room. Géza helped by calling out cold, lukewarm, warm and finally hot as I happily popped the delicacy into my mouth. I looked forward to this little game. Mother told me later that the chocolate was really a vitamin bar. I thought she was pulling my leg. I have no idea where Uncle Géza got it from, or if it was really a vitamin bar. Presumably he stocked up on it before the war and doled it out one square at a time with great drama to entertain and treat his great niece, me.

Aranka left no impression on me. Everyone else, my mother, grandmother and my Aunt Ibi, always called her "a witch without a broom." I don't remember any of her petty tirades that I heard about, but in retrospect, feel very sorry for her. It couldn't have been easy to suddenly share her gracious home overlooking the Danube with six adults and two children. The menagerie consisted of her husband's sister and her husband, their daughter Iréne and her three year old daughter, me, Iréne's two sisters-in-law, one with a thirteen year old boy, and Iréne's mother-in-law. All this with the frightful din of war playing in the background! Gyurika, Aranka's mentally retarded son, was already dead and the other one, the dashing handsome Pista, out somewhere on the Russian front, if he was still alive. Everything she valued was in a shambles, and this awful assembly of hodgepodge relatives has demanded she part with her last possession, a jar of poppy seeds sitting atop her wardrobe. They couldn't comprehend why she wanted to hold onto that while they were all starving. They couldn't understand how important it was to her to have it for Pista's return, so she can make him his favourite poppy seed noodles. For return, he must. She couldn't bear to think about the alternative. If only the bombing would stop!

Most apartment buildings in Budapest are U-shaped, built around a central stairwell. The gang —short for gangway— connects the entrances of two to five apartments on a floor. The gang usually has wrought iron railings, similar to a balcony. The apartment buildings are normally three to six stories high, so the building casts a shadow on its courtyard and much of the gang. In most of the courtyards, a lone tree stretches its arms longingly toward the open sky and the light that penetrates into the dingy enclosure from three to six stories above. Even grass and weeds think better of trying to survive these conditions, resulting in utterly barren ground around the poor tree. The gang was where children hung out, ostensibly to get some sunshine and fresh air; neighbours exchanged gossip, and old people sat to watch the comings and goings. In reality, the gang had everything, except fresh air. Instead, it had stale cooking odours, mixed with the smell of garbage coming from the small wooden boxes sitting in front of each apartment, blended with trapped city fumes and the scent of lye soap the vice-super used to scrub the stairs and the gang.

My first cohesive memory is of the gang at my Aunt Böske's apartment where we moved to as soon as the battle was over. I took my dolls out there in their pram, dressed them, talked to them and pretended we were in a park or expecting a visitor. From time to time, I also pretended there was an air-raid and we had to hurry to get the blankets to go to the air-raid shelter. I clearly remember —I must have been about three and a half years old— playing on the gang in front of the apartment, when a burning stench reached my nose. The odour was coming from the open window of Aunt Böske's kitchen, an offensive intrusion into the pleasant peace of my morning playtime. My mother and Aunt Böske were making kukorica málé and somehow managed to burn it. An odd memory to have vividly survived, while others faded into nothingness.

Right after the war, in the spring of 1945, my two aunts, Böske's and Ibi, and my mother zealously scoured the city to find any food to feed the nine of us. They were imaginative in preparing whatever they could get, trying to make the meals as good as possible, but there was one memorable culinary disaster when they had tried to make the malé, a sweet corn bread. We never saw the cornmeal creation, and both of them walked around with long faces for the rest of the day. This was a near tragedy, because the cornmeal had been a triumphant find in the starving city.

———

Róbert and his wife Eva saved my father's letters for decades. When Róbert passed away, Eva went on what I called her "archaeological digs" in their London apartment and found many letters from my father, mother and my grandmother. The ones from my father, of course, are the most meaningful. To hear him describe in his own words how he felt about me and his concerns for his family is an unbelievably great gift to me. He was an excellent writer, clearly expressing his feelings without holding back, drama or formality. He must have felt very close to my Uncle Róbert to have been able to so openly voice his concerns. I'm forever grateful to Eva for finding them and taking the trouble to get them into my hands. God bless you!

My father's words seem familiar. Reading his letters, I feel the stirrings of forgotten memories — memories that, for years, my mother had firmly told everyone I didn't have. Her words echo in my mind: "She can't remember anything about her father. She was too young when he was called up." As a dutiful daughter, I took her word for it and didn't remember, until these letters, a gift precious beyond description, reached me and told me otherwise. Mother usually simplified problems she didn't know how to solve. She didn't know how to approach my feelings, so she simply decided there was nothing to worry about. The fact that such a statement negated the pain I felt, for which I had no words to express, never occurred to my mother nor any of the other adults I knew. They were busy licking their own wounds and the thought of their children not experiencing that pain gave them comfort.

Even more recently, while scanning old black and white pictures for a family album CD, as I looked at a photo I've seen a million times before. Suddenly I could see the color of my father's jacket and smell the mixture of tobacco and Diana, an aromatic alcohol-based home remedy, my father used as an aftershave, emanating from it. I checked with my cousin Tomi and he confirmed the memory was indeed correct, despite being buried in my subconscious for nearly six decades.

Rózsi and Vilmos ca. 1942

Liberation

Another hazy image in my recollection is that of the Russian soldiers coming into the makeshift air raid shelter in the basement of Uncle Géza's apartment building. The occupants of the shelter greeted their entry with fear, joy, suspicion and relief. The war was over. But what would be the price? The German propaganda machine had successfully painted the Russians as a barbaric horde. While I heard accounts, as an adult, that indicated some of the Russians were uncouth, drinking, raping and pillaging, all my personal experiences were positive.

As soon as it was possible, we, the unwanted guests, left Uncle Géza's and moved to Aunt Böske's apartment a few blocks away. Mother told me she covered my pram with a blanket during this short trip, so I wouldn't see human and animal corpses protruding from the snow banks. Afterward, for several days, maybe weeks, I stayed in the apartment. My mother was afraid to take me out with her, because in addition to the gruesome sights, spent and unexploded ammunition littered the streets.

The day I got out into the open street was a great adventure for me. The boulevard teemed with people and the sun was shining. Russian soldiers, driving large trucks filled to the brim with big, unwrapped loaves of black bread, stopped at street corners and, smiling, placed half-loaves into people's outstretched hands. I can still see the hundreds of hands reaching toward the truck. Old and young stood ten deep, waiting patiently for their turn. When Mother and I got close enough, I stretched out my tiny hands too and said kleba —Russian for bread— as I had heard others say. The soldier jumped off his truck with a full loaf in his hand, squatted beside me, brushed his rough hand over my hair, called me djevochka —"little girl"— and handed me a whole loaf. That day I was the provider for the family, still living at my aunt's —nine people cramped into a three-room apartment. I was three and a half and had spent a large portion of my life going to the air raid shelter, eating the ever-decreasing rations of beans, peas, lentils and wheat gruel, washed down with cold unsweetened tea. After the fighting stopped, early in 1945, there was no food in the city. The roads, bridges and railway lines were in tatters and the capital cut off even from the bits of stored food that remained in the countryside. I heard many tales of people going down to the street and carving out chunks of meat from horses killed during the house-to-house battle of Budapest. Our own apartment was uninhabitable. Fairly early in the battle of Budapest, perhaps in the fall of 1944, an Allied bomb had hit a hospital a block away. The Germans were using the hospital, clearly marked with a large red cross on the roof, to store ammunition and land mines. Allied intelligence discovered this fact and targeted the building. When the bombs hit the hospital, the detonation blew out all the windows for several square blocks; the walls dividing the five apartments on the top floor in our building collapsed, burying all the furnishings under a pile of rubble. The building had several holes where shrapnel penetrated the plaster, the corner of the top floor wraparound terrace was missing, several balconies were hanging by the iron reinforcement bars, and the plaster ceiling decorations–angels, flowers, and curlicues–dangled in the elegantly designed entrance hall, broken to bits, prevented from falling by the wire mesh originally used as a base to create them.

The city authorities set up to deal with the acute housing crisis assigned us to an immense apartment a block away from our former home. It had three rooms of oversized proportions, a long hallway, a big kitchen and a maid's room. The ceilings were thirteen feet high. My maternal grandparents, grandmother's cousin Frida —Nene to me— mother and I moved into these cavernous rooms. Mother used to joke that you needed hiking boots just to go to the kitchen from the living room. The apartment was on the third floor, and fuel for heating had to be carried from the basement locker. There was a floor-to-ceiling ceramic stove in the center room, used as a living room, but the adjoining rooms got heat only if the interconnecting doors were open. Fuel was a precious commodity, so this seldom happened. The rest of the apartment —bedrooms, kitchen and bathroom— was frigid. The windows had no glass and, until manufacturing and distribution could be re-established, people secured brown wrapping paper in place of the missing panes and shellacked the paper to make it less opaque. The wind rattling the brittle paper provided a constant background noise. From the bombing and shelling, large chunks of plaster had fallen out of the spaces where brick met the wooden window frames, so the wind entered through the cracks and whistled through the whole apartment. We were lucky to be able to heat one room. Under these circumstances, the once elegant bay window was no advantage at all. It was only more window area where the elements conspired against making the place cozy.

Usually, my mother heated a basin of water on the kitchen stove and washed me in it in the relatively warm living room.. The adults braved the ice-cold bathroom to wash in cold water. Taking a real bath was a full evening's production. The bathroom had a big water tank that used wood for fuel. Grandfather started the fire a couple of hours before the event. The tank also heated the otherwise freezing room. After the bath, my mother or my grandfather would carry me, wrapped in a blanket, to the heated living room to put on my nightgown and housecoat.

Mother dusted the perimeter of each room with DDT daily to try to control the hordes of bedbugs that infested almost all dwellings in the city. She was determined to eradicate the pests after she found one morning our sheets covered with spots of blood from bedbugs crushed under our bodies. She also treated the back of all the paintings with the bug remedy and sealed them with brown paper. Aided by Nene, mother spread DDT around the room in white clouds of dust. Using what looked like a giant saltshaker, they turned over armchairs and sofa to give them a dose of the deadly powder, too. The smell of shellac and DDT permeated the whole apartment.

To this discord of unpleasant odours, mother added the smell of gasoline when she discovered I had head lice. She washed my hair in gas and there I sat, my head wrapped in a towel, smelling like a gas station for what seemed like hours. Then she unwrapped me, sat me on a chair on top of a layer of newspapers and combed my tangled hair with a fine-tooth louse comb. I cried and complained as she yanked, while her action whipped my head this way and that, but she ignored my protests. Her satisfaction came with the ever-increasing number of black dots on the newsprint, signifying dead lice and her triumph over the enemy. She retold the tale of the lice battle for years afterward. Every time I heard it, I squirmed with guilt and embarrassment, as if I had been somehow responsible for placing myself in that predicament and putting her to all that trouble.

My grandfather had advanced Alzheimer's disease—they called it calcification of the arteries of the brain at that time—and just about the only skill he had left was to build the fire in the great tiled stove that occupied a corner of the center room. He patiently crumpled paper for the grate, carefully placed slivers of wood on top and lighted it. At just the crucial moment, he placed a larger piece of wood on top and blew until it caught fire. He guarded his fire all day, to make sure it burned in the most efficient way possible.

Grandfather was a very handsome old gentleman. He was seventy-three and taller than average for a Hungarian. Whenever I think of him, I see his slim, erect figure, the chain of his pocket watch draped across his vest; a tall man with a shock of white hair, and a kindly, albeit confused look in his china-blue eyes, hidden behind round-rimmed tortoiseshell glasses. I couldn't understand why everyone was upset with him. To me, he seemed perfectly normal. He was my playmate, happily building castles from toy blocks or showing off the treasures he stored in his pockets. We probably were the same mental age at that point. His pockets were always full of wonderful things: bits of string, old buttons, an old watch fob, coloured paper, wooden matches and an old hooked shoe buttoner. They served to create a toy or a game for us at a moment's notice. It was fascinating to see just what he had and what he could make of it. The button on a string was my favourite. He could make it spin so a humming sound emanated from it, making me giggle. He made this simple toy by putting a string through each of two holes in a large button, tying the ends together, then held the string in both hands with the button dangling in the middle as he wound the string with a circular motion. When it was wound up, he pulled the string tight, which made the button whirl and hum.

Every morning, I did up the laces on grandfather's high-top shoes and he thanked me. Each night, he held up my quilt to the stove to warm it, then wrapped me in it and carried me to my bed. He called me "Kicsike" —little one— and had the softest look in his blue eyes when he looked at me. A year or two later, when he moved into a nursing home, somehow our bond broke. In those sterile surroundings, I couldn't relate to my playmate and he probably didn't know how to amuse me in that situation. Instead, when we visited him, he spent the whole time sitting beside me, addressing me in the familiar way as "Kicsike" and stroking my hair.

One day, my grandmother and mother took me to the zoo. Although some of the buildings had damage, and I presume some of the animals had perished, it was open to the public. As soon as I saw the little carriage drawn by a dwarf pony, I wanted to ride in it. Being four, I didn't understand that the carriage belonged to the photographer and you had to pay for the photos to have the ride, a short trip around the zoo. The price was a sum, far beyond our means. When my begging met with a firm no, I threw a tantrum. Two very young Russian soldiers came over, wanting to know what was wrong with the djevochka. Mother explained in pantomime that I wanted a pony ride, but we had no money. Before my tears dried, strong hands lifted me onto the seat behind the pony and I found myself wedged between the two young men to ride around the zoo. From my perch, I looked around triumphantly, like a queen, beaming at the other children who gaped in envy at my good luck. The photographer took the two pictures the Russians had paid for and printed them. They kept one copy and handed the other to my mother. Prompted by Mother, I thanked them profusely. I still have the picture; it's among my most prized possession. I often wonder where the second picture is now and how those soldiers remember that incident; when far from home, perhaps missing desperately their own children or siblings, they had made a little girl very happy.

During most of 1945, to feed the family, mother traded her jewellery for food. Luckily, she had plenty of pieces that had no sentimental value; my father had bought them at auctions before the war for just such a situation. She went down to the Western Railroad Station, a few blocks away, and traded a ring for a sack of flour, wood for the stove or a basket of potatoes. The currency had no value; farmers traded for goods such as jewellery and saved the items for themselves or traded it for what they needed. I heard many stories of farmers proudly displaying a valuable clock or a large radio among their rough furnishings. Often they had no electricity in their house for the radio, so it sat there as an ornament, unused.

One night, Nene brought home a large tin of meat she had obtained somewhere. It was a wondrous thing. We sat around the table in expectant awe as grandfather's nimble fingers worked the little key around the can. Mother reverently sliced the meat and placed a chunk on each plate. In silence, we savoured the treat. It was the most delicious thing I'd ever had.

Most kids and adults too, in the city of Budapest, were severely malnourished during the war and had multiple health problems from the tainted water, lack of sanitation and a variety of epidemics that swept through the weakened population. As soon as the Children's Hospital was open, in the summer of 1945, Mother took me for a check-up. Every other parent in Budapest must have had the same desire to have their children's health checked out, because there was a considerable crowd. To use the doctor's time efficiently, benches were set up along the wall in a long hallway and dozens of children sat in a row, stripped to the waist as ordered by the nurse. Then kindly old Dr. Leitner appeared with his stethoscope and examined each of us in turn. On Dr. Leitner's recommendation, I enrolled in a kindergarten the Red Cross operated. It was a pleasant place with a sandbox and swings, but for my mother its major attraction was the nutritious hot meal they served at midday. At least Mother could stop worrying about getting the right kind of food for a growing child. It was in this kindergarten that I first tasted real meat in a gulash served at lunch, and went home to ask my mother why she never cooked the stuff. As one can imagine, that remark cut her to the bone!

———

The canned meat stayed in my memory as something truly delicious and special. It wasn't until I came to Canada that I tasted that flavour again when I opened a can of Spam.
    I always keep a button on a string handy to amuse little ones who come to visit my home.

Eva with Russian soldiers, 1945

Everyday Life

Changing Times

When the city cleared some of the rubble and life started to take close to normal shape, my mother tried to take my father's place in the automotive parts wholesale partnership he had founded with his brother, Gyula. It was a difficult task. She had no marketable skills. She was, as was the custom of her day and social status, educated in the social graces rather than in subjects that would help her earn a living. She was fluent in German, had taken conversational French from the Paris-born wife of an aristocrat, played the piano and did embroidery. This was hardly the résumé she needed to deal with the employees and the stockroom of an auto parts business. In addition, Gyula was a hard taskmaster. In the past, he had shared his worries and the day-to-day decision-making with his brother. He missed that deeply, especially as his frustration with his sister-in-law's lack of skills and her unwillingness to adapt grew by the day.

As soon as she realized she had to make a living and be responsible, Iréne cast around for a new husband. She explained this to me in detail, although I was less than five. Her philosophy of childrearing was to be a girlfriend to me rather than a mother. She discussed whatever was on her mind as we went shopping or for a walk. She also made it clear that if I disagreed with her decision to remarry, I'd feel guilty when I married and had a home, leaving her lonely in her old age. With my father gone, she was my responsibility now and I was going to rise to that job. I started taking on responsibilities far beyond the competence of my age.

While my mother tried to learn the inner workings of a business, political times were changing. Gyula was worried. If the communists were to gain power in the elections of 1947, he'd have to evaluate the consequences on business and make adjustments. My mother was unable to offer support or be a sounding board to his thoughts. She had no knowledge of politics and didn't want to learn about it.

She was in her element when she prepared for the annual Automotive Association Ball, though. Before the war, the Ball was a very elegant affair and the highlight of the social season. Once the war was over, the members wanted to reinstate it early, as if to say, "Everything is normal." My mother needed something to wear. Buying a new dress would have been out of the question, both because of the cost and because most likely nothing suitable would have been available in the stores. Merchants could barely keep up with stocking necessities. Formal wear wasn't a high priority.

After a long discussion, following mother's pirouetting through the living room, modeling every dress she owned, they decided her black dress redecorated would have to do. This was the consensus of the three adult women in the home: my mother, my grandmother and Nene. My grandfather and I were mere spectators without a vote in this drama. The decoration was to be a couple of rows of brass tacks usually used for holding documents together, pressed into the fabric just above the hem. This mundane office supply became art under my grandmother's talented fingers as she pressed each one through the cloth and bent the stems back to hold it in place. The project took several evenings and I sat in mute fascination as her hands magically created a glittering ball gown from the simple black dress.

The only problem now was that the dress was very heavy, but mother would bravely carry it through the ball. Uncle Gyula, dressed in his pre-war tuxedo, accompanied her to the great event. The Communist Minister of Transportation, Ernö Gerö, keynote speaker for the evening, showed up in a factory workers' beige shirt, open at the neck, to deliver his speech. The garb of the minister was a clear message that the workers would dictate business now, not this spoilt overdressed group of bourgeois. Mother was scandalized for days. Uncle Gyula commented wryly: "How outgoing of him!" but the handwriting of things to come was on the wall.

Mother was exhausted all the time, trying to live up to
Gyula's demands, even though she only worked until about two in
the afternoon. Grandfather had to be institutionalized because he
could no longer safely stay at home alone due to his worsening
Alzheimer's disease. Grandmother and her cousin, Nene,
reopened the necktie store.

I went to kindergarten in the morning and was dropped off
at the Koháry Restaurant at one o'clock by the kindergarten
teacher. The Koháry Restaurant, a no-frills eatery in the basement
of our old apartment building, was to me the ultimate in security.
It was a family operation. The staff consisted of Annus Néni, the
cook; her daughter, the dwarf cashier; and another family member
as waitress. I had known the three of them all of my short life.

I arrived, greeted the dwarf cashier, surveyed the scene
from the top of the steps and then headed to the kitchen to
retrieve my booster cushion and the small cutlery set that was set
aside, right by the door, just for me. A quick survey of the kitchen
showed enormous pots with steaming food. An incongruous
mixture of aromas—frying onions, vanilla, roasting meat and
copious amounts of garlic—mixed in the steam-laden air. I waved
to Annus Néni, the conductor of this symphony, bent over one of
her pots, beads of perspiration on her forehead from the
suffocating heat. Careful to stay out of the way of the waitress
carrying platters of food, I took my equipment to a seat I'd chosen
in my preliminary survey of the room, usually next to some
friendly-looking diner. Long tables, covered in worn oilcloth,
seating up to ten people, jutted out from each side of the room
against the peeling walls. People sat wherever they found an open
spot on a bench.

While patrons could order à la carte, most people chose one
of the two daily specials that included soup, entrée, and dessert.
Some had prepaid weekly meal tickets at a discount. The place was
always packed, and several people hovered near the kitchen
entrance with food carriers, a contraption of matching aluminium
pots held together with two strips of metal ending in a handle, for
take-out service. People chatted freely with their neighbours and

the whole atmosphere was that of a club especially formed to partake of the cooking skills of the rotund Annus Néni.

The waitress treated me like an adult, listing the foods I could choose from the prepaid options, and in turn, I ordered what I pleased from her list. The soups were simple, made with preserved tomatoes, green peas, caraway seeds and croutons, or my favourite, egg-drop soup with bay leaves. Some of them had homemade dumplings of egg and flour, as tradition dictated. The foods I best remember were the vegetables in white sauce, especially garlicky spinach topped with either a piece of roast pork, a hamburger patty, a fried egg or a savoury variation on French toast. Potato casserole made with hardboiled eggs, sausage and plenty of sour cream was, and remains to this day, my favourite dish. For dessert, I loved the cottage cheese dumplings and the plum-filled potato dumplings that were light, yet oozing with sugar and cinnamon. Nudli, small torpedoes of potato dough drenched in browned breadcrumbs and sprinkled with sugar, were superb, too. Annus Néni prepared all her food with much care and consistency to show her love for her many devoted customers. While waiting for the food to arrive, I talked with my neighbours at the table. I never noticed I was the only unaccompanied child in the room. By two o'clock, the crowd had thinned. If my mother was late, I joined the staff on the back stoop, shelling peas with them and joining in their conversation. Since I loved them all and felt their reciprocated warmth, being left with Annus Néni and her crew was no hardship at all.

To this day, the memory of the wonderful food Annus Néni created in her kitchen inspires my cooking, and I try to emulate her attitude of expressing love for my diners through the care in my food preparation.

———

Most of the customers in the restaurant were men. I found out much later that they were lawyers and judges from the nearby courts. When I was twenty-one, I was introduced to one of these men in Canada.

He recognized me from way back then. I found out from him that I tremendously amused the patrons with my poise and independence.

Annus Néni's kitchen was nationalized in the early 50's, along with all the other businesses, large and small. The little restaurant is still there, now in private hands again. They jazzed it up with tables for four, some decorations, pretensions and higher prices, but somehow the flavour remains. Or is it the memories emanating from the walls that play tricks on me?

Eva in front of apartment, 1948

Peace Hotel

I think for most people in Europe, the war was so incomprehensible that they shut it away, as you push a file you cannot quite deal with to the back of the desk, in hopes that the problems in it will solve themselves with time. It was either that or insanity. While many did go mad or had stress-related illnesses, surprisingly, the great majority went on as if nothing happened.

The best example was the Béke Kávéház, a coffeehouse on Teréz Körút, near the Western Railroad station. The körút or boulevard was later renamed Lenin Körút. It was the summer of 1946, only a year after the Russian soldiers found us cowering like beaten animals in the basements of shell-pocked apartment buildings, shyly reaching out for their offerings of kleba and chay —bread and tea. The Béke Kávéház had become a meeting place for the young, thirty to forty year olds, widows and widowers, who congregated there to seek new partners in the hope of rebuilding their lives and restoring its prewar harmony. Poignantly, béke means peace in the Hungarian language.

In the café, the "Five O'clock Tea" was in full swing. A man could ask a woman to dance without formal introduction, which was the requirement of propriety. Eligible widowers sat alone or in small groups, eyeing the array of Budapest's widows.

A *garde dame* —chaperone— accompanied the widows as if they were still sixteen-year-old debutantes. The garde dame, usually an elderly female relative, was dressed in formal black, as befitted her age and the important decorum of her function. A fresh white *jabot* —something resembling a frilly ascot— and white, crocheted gloves were the only indication she wasn't in mourning. The younger women, freshly groomed, wore light-coloured, lightweight afternoon party dresses, often remodelled

from a relic of their former affluent prewar days, or had a new
dress made from an old curtain by a skilful seamstress. Gold
jewellery dripped from arms, neck and earlobes, as much gold as
the entire extended family could muster, to give the best possible
impression of the widow's wealth, so she could land a good match.

A six-piece band played Benny Goodman, Tommy Dorsey
and Glen Miller, as if they had just stepped out of a Ginger Rogers
and Fred Astaire movie, the trombones sliding up and down,
glimmering, and wire brushes scraping the drums. Children
sometimes accompanied the widows, but usually another older
female relative whisked them off, after a brief treat of pastry and a
sugar cube dipped in hot, strong espresso, so the widow wouldn't
look too encumbered.

We had to look hard for signs that a devastating war was
only a year past. The sooty, peeling walls of the café, the broken
plaster cherubs on the ceiling, the threadbare tuxedos of the
musicians, the chipped marble tables were easily overlooked. The
fact that the hotel above was mostly ruined, an empty shell held
up by scaffolding, went unnoticed. It wasn't unusual. Scaffolding
held together most of Budapest. On a windy day, you had to be
alert, watching out for flying plaster, roof tiles, or pieces of sharp
tin windowsills. Café patrons ignored the apartment building
across the street that sported several major holes from the intense
house-to-house street battles of a year before. The building, with
its Victorian balconies drooping as if they were melted plastic and
not stone and wrought iron, and its eaves hanging at precarious
angles, stood there as a silent witness to the violence of the war,
but no one looked at it. After all, they would tell themselves, there
were positive changes. The shellacked wrapping-paper windows
were slowly replaced by real glass. The number six streetcar rattled
past from time to time, clanging on rickety rails. And the orchestra
played "Stardust."

The widowers glowed, pink-skinned from their fresh close
shave. Those from the countryside arrived by train at the nearby
railroad station earlier in the day, cleaned up and preened at a
hotel or in a relative's apartment. The males were fully aware of
their importance as eligible men. The supply was so short that

even these country bumpkins with two left feet and lack of refined graces had no problem getting dance partners. After surveying the field of women, one would rise, cross the floor with as much dignity as his too-tight tweed suit would allow, bow deeply in front of the chosen lady and ask: "May I have this dance?" One or two numbers later, he guided her back to her table, thanked her, and bowed to the garde dame, just as he would have in 1935.

There, in this café, the war years didn't exist. The men revelled in the bantering of these women dressed in their best afternoon party dresses as if they were still teenagers at the prom. Similarly, their dancing partners went back to the garde dame to report on how good or bad a match each man seemed to be, giggling like debutantes over his looks. Sometimes, the dance led to more dances or even dates, and the dates often led to marriage proposals. There was no drawn-out courtship or engagement. If compatible, they made marriage plans before the couple grew to know each other. The sense of urgency to restore things to normal and the need to feel secure overrode caution.

The men from Budapest itself were even more scarce than males from the country were, and behaved differently. They donned again their well-known suave, sophisticated, devil-may-care attitude and dropped in briefly so the women would admire and desire them, but soon rushed off for a "business appointment." They could afford to be haughty. For each of them, there were ten women who jumped for a bit of attention. Many of these men were engaged in black-marketeering. They were invigorated by the danger of living on the edge, and determined to prove to the world and themselves they were worthy of having survived. With their high earnings, they were able to provide for the remainders of their decimated families: mothers' aunts, elderly uncles, cousins. Surviving hadn't been an accident; they were Titans, capable of everything.

Politics were almost never discussed. Béke —peace— had returned, and the sun shone. That the peace was as fragile as the scaffolds around the Hotel named after it went unnoticed. This menagerie sat gossiping, drinking espresso, eating ice cream from a silvery dish, one scoop each of chocolate, vanilla and strawberry, or a pastry with whipped cream.

I personally preferred the five o'clock tea at the Emke coffeehouse, but of course, no one ever asked a five year old. Once in a while, Mother decided to go there to see if the eligible men were more interesting than at the Béke. The Emke was further down the boulevard, next to the imposing National Theatre. The interior was dark and told of a more elegant era, but most important to me, it had a floorshow; a cabaret where jugglers, singers, magicians and dancers, clad in colourful costumes, followed each other in quick succession on the small stage. I sat enthralled by the grace of dancing girls in scanty sequined outfits, loved the throaty, mellow songs of the chanteuse, and was totally in awe of the magician who pulled paper flowers from an empty hat.

———

The National Theatre is gone now. In its place, a landscaped green area is home to a variety of vendors, hurrying pedestrians rushing to catch the metro or a streetcar. The Emke Hotel has been restored; the café, remodelled, is now a German-style beer parlour.

I knew one of the self-important black-marketeering single men who came and went at the Béke in 1946. He was a distant relative and was most desirable —very handsome and a bachelor. He could have picked any of the eligible women there, but eventually chose to marry a very homely woman instead. He spent the rest of his life being an extremely jealous husband.

The Béke Hotel is now the Radisson, fully refurbished with plush carpets and silently gliding, liveried staff. The place where the coffeehouse was is now a glitzy gift shop, but right above on the next floor is the very beautiful Zsolnay Kávéház, a café, with the ambience of the 19th century pastry shops. A pianist plays the haunting songs of yesteryear every afternoon, while the elderly patrons, some of them likely the same ones who came to the afternoon teas after the war, sit and gossip over coffee with whipped cream and slices of masterfully created tortes. It's one of my favourite places to meet friends.

Last spring as I was waiting for my friends in the Zsolnay, I overheard an interesting conversation from the next table. A woman in her late seventies sat with a young man. He was explaining something intently to her. I didn't pay much attention to them, until her voice rose. "Just make it ring! At my age, I don't respond to tunes. If it's a telephone, it should ring!" I surmised the young man was a grandson, setting a cellular telephone and teaching Grandma how to use it. In the meantime, the elderly pianist played "Stardust".

Rózsi and Eva 1947

Nationalizations

My mother was unable to cope with the demands of the wholesale business and Uncle Gyula. Uncle Gyula bought out my father's share of the partnership and Mother left the business. According to the law, I was my father's rightful heir and, until I reached the age of majority, the government appointed a Public Trustee to manage these funds on my behalf. Mother got a small allowance for my keep, extra for clothing and other necessities and, with proof of purchase, could also start collecting items for my trousseau.

While this solved her unrelenting problems of fighting with Uncle Gyula, Mother was insecure. She had no actual marketable skills other than her experience in dealing with customers in my grandmother's store. Clerking in a store wouldn't keep us alive, especially in the style she liked. She was used to having a maid to do the heavier housework, money for custom-made clothes, shoes and hats, as well as enough time on her hands to meet her friends in coffee shops one or two afternoons a week. The only solution for her was to remarry to recapture the support of a good provider and regain the comforts she had lost.

Zoli was all that. He was a kind widower of means who was prepared to have her as the lady of his country manor and be a father to me. To this end, he legally adopted me. In the meantime, the chasm that started with the conflict with Uncle Gyula and, according to my mother, continued when the other members of my father's family refused to support her against him, grew to the point where I was forbidden to recognize my paternal grandmother on the street. Being a very young child, I understood little of the conflict and I did as I was told.

Zoli owned a steam mill and farm near Debrecen, about

two hundred kilometres from Budapest. He spent most of his time running the farm and mill, while Mother stayed in the city. As the wife of a country squire, Mother was in her element. She ordered several new outfits from her tailor and new custom-made clothes for me from a very an expensive children's couturier. Then, she looked up all her old friends, inviting them to meet for coffee and pastry so she could tell them of her great fortune. Next, she made a deal to exchange the temporary apartment for one in the building where we had lived before the war and sent the furniture off to be reupholstered.

Looking back, Zoli had great and progressive ideas of agriculture. He bought Yorkshire and Berkshire pigs from England to raise and to breed. These animals produced more meat and less fat than the longhaired Hungarian pigs that were the customary farm animal. He felt there was a better market for the lean meat. To feed the pigs, he cooked the waste bran from the mill with potatoes from his fields that weren't marketable in great cauldrons. He established a small still to produce schnapps from the fruit that fell off the trees in his and his neighbour's orchards. He was energetic and innovative, and since he was always fair to his workers, the landless peasants, he was a very popular man in his district.

A wave of nationalizations started in 1948, a few months after the Communists took power. First, the major conglomerates of heavy industry fell under the axe. Slogans posted everywhere reinforced the party line: "The factory is yours, you are working for yourself!" It was only a matter of time before the large agricultural holdings became a target and were taken away from the owners by the government. Zoli did some legal manoeuvring to change the mill into a cooperative, sharing the ownership with his workers to stave off nationalization for a while. My mother managed to convince the Public Trustee to invest my inheritance into Zoli's farm, thinking that surely they wouldn't rob an underage child of her funds by nationalizing her investment. I became the legal owner of the large estate house and the farmyard surrounding it, complete with the little pink and black pigs and the still. Of course, I had no idea what it meant. I vaguely knew, from catching snippets of conversation around me, that I had money deposited with the public trustee that came from my father's business, and that my mother collected sums from the trustee for my keep. I felt loved by Zoli, enjoyed the farm on summer holidays with my mother, and the plenitude of good food Zoli brought with him to the city on weekends.

Zoli was good to me. At the farm, during school holidays, he introduced me to his workers, neighbours and relatives, with pride, as his daughter. I soaked up the unfamiliar country atmosphere. The baking of bread in the communal oven fascinated me. I had breakfasts of rich, hot chocolate with fresh bread and cheese under the great walnut tree in the front yard. I swam in the moat surrounding the mill; we went to the fields when the thresher arrived and watched as the sheaves of wheat were fed in one end and the grain flowed into the sacks at the other. Then we trudged home through the stubble alive with red poppies and blue cornflowers, the hot sun beating down on us until we reached the shade of the mulberry tree at the far end of the estate yard. I had a dog, Csöpi, to play with during the lazy summer afternoons. I also had a pet goat. Her antics provided further entertainment. I never knew what she would do next. Her best trick was to jump through the open window of the living room on a hot day and lie down on the sofa in the cool, shaded room.

Zoli, Mother and I took trips to Debrecen, where we lunched in the elegance of the ballroom of the Bika Hotel, then went to the swimming pool for the afternoon or shopped and went sightseeing in town. The highlight of my stay was the Festival of New Bread. A parade started the festivities. The first float was an open farm cart pulled by horses and decorated with flowers. A young woman in her best embroidered country costume stood on it and held up the oversized loaf, baked from the first flour of the mill that year, for all to see. A noisy band followed the cart, carriages of dignitaries in their Sunday best behind that, and finally a flock of gypsies in their colourful garb on foot. The destination was one of the estates, where we had a communal meal at long tables. There was lots of wine, music, singing, great tubs of food and good cheer all around. The whole village must have been invited. I was six years old and didn't know it was to be my last chance to witness the magic of the Festival of New Bread.

The steamroller of nationalization didn't stop. One by one, the smaller enterprises fell to the Communist program expansion. Uncle Gyula lost his wholesale business when the nationalizations extended to companies with fewer than ten employees. They closed the business and made an apartment out of the premises. He had to get a job in a state-run truck manufacturing firm, where some of his expertise was useful. Daily, news reached us through the grapevine of friends and relatives losing their property and livelihood. The inevitable happened: the mill fell under the nationalization hatchet and so did the farm with its house and yard —appropriated by the government without any compensation to the owners. The law had no sympathy for the holdings of a child. Zoli became bookkeeper at the central food distribution firm, *Közért,* and moved to Budapest permanently. His former workers reluctantly joined the collective farm that now had its offices in the house I owned. Occasionally they visited, bringing a small parcel of food and a lot of sympathy for the squire. Zoli wasn't unhappy in his new job, but the pay was low. Mother had to find a way to help with the expenses. She decided to take out a license for a home occupation and start a stocking mending business in our apartment.

Since nylons were scarce and expensive, most of them smuggled or slipped into letters from the west, there was brisk business in fixing the runs in them. First, she had to catch the intact loop of the stitch at the end of the run, using a delicate hook attached to a small hose from an intermittent compressed air machine that drove the hook up and down. The mechanized hook lifted the loop and drew it through each rung of the ladder. The runs disappeared and were fastened in position with a fine thread. This was the same process as when a knitter recovers a dropped stitch with a crochet hook, but mechanized and in miniature. Mother had great dexterity and she mastered the skill in no time. It was backbreaking work for her, bending over the cup that held the stocking and watching the fine threads whiz by under the strong light. Since she couldn't obtain fine enough thread for this purpose, she unravelled old stockings. The job of unravelling the nylons and spooling the thread was my job. Unfortunately, stocking repair was seasonal, because people didn't wear stockings in the summer, so mother also started painting aprons, handkerchiefs and silk scarves. Zoli brought home his coworkers' stockings to fix and carried Mother's art to work to sell to these same coworkers, while the small sign in the entranceway of our apartment building and word-of-mouth brought a steady clientele for Mother's crafts.

The tax collector was a frequent visitor, putting a lean against a Persian rug or an oil painting for taxes in arrears. Mother somehow always scraped together the taxes before the deadline, often by selling a piece of jewellery.

In the evenings, friends or neighbours popped into our apartment to discuss politics in hushed tones, such as the war in Indochina or the Kuomintang. They often listened to Radio Free Europe or the Voice of America crackling through the airwaves. Zoli and Mother told me never to repeat anything I heard at these gatherings and I never did —especially because I didn't understand any of what they discussed.

Goods in the stores, including foodstuffs, all but disappeared. Mother and Grandmother bemoaned the lack of oranges and bananas, but I couldn't sympathize since I'd never tasted them. Where it mattered to me was that everyone started to take lard sandwiches, the traditional poor man's fare, to school for lunch, but since I couldn't swallow that stuff, I had to convince my mother to give me jam sandwiches instead. The jam came in big, long blocks the consistency of patè, and the clerk sliced off a bit to wrap in waxed paper. Rumour had it that the "jam" never saw fruit and was made of rotten tomatoes. I never knew the truth of that. Its taste was acceptable to me.

We were very lucky if we could get a bit of meat once a week. All kinds of odd recipes sprang up. People made orange cake from carrots, almond paste from wheatlets with apricot pits for flavouring. Mother made sardines from smelts and cooking oil by a laborious process, and this new creative culinary art form produced a tasty meal from the cow udder that was occasionally available in the meat market.

The huge, tiled butcher shop, once full of raw meat and smoked hams hanging from massive metal hooks, was empty, save for the big block of lard presiding over the middle. The five clerks idly ambled up and down, commiserating with the odd customer who happened by. Commiserating had to be done very carefully, and only with a trusted customer, when they were alone. Vigorous complaining could reach the ears of the Party and could result in being persecuted for being a reactionary and land you in jail.

To the surprise of my classmates and me, one New Years' Eve afternoon —we must have been about twelve— we received an invitation to a children's ball in the magnificent parliament building. I asked my mother, as soon as I knew of it, to allow me to go. She promised to take me. For weeks, my classmates and I were in a fever pitch of excitement, talking about what we were going to wear and who might be there. It was an all-girl school — most schools in Hungary separated the boys and the girls— and we had recently started taking interest in boys. This was, so to speak, our coming-out dance. We, a group of close friends, arranged to meet when we got there. I was excited and looking forward to this special event.

As we started off on foot toward the parliament building in the December fog, which is so typical of Hungarian winters, Mother announced she was tired of Zoli living off her labour and she was getting a divorce. She asked if I minded. The fog from the outside wrapped itself around my heart. What could I say? I couldn't make her decisions for her. I didn't want her to stay in a marriage because I was comfortable with Zoli as a father. I told her I would go along with her decision. I was numb. I could no longer think of the dance, but I couldn't deal with this news, either.

Silently, we reached the parliament building, entered the foyer blazing with light from the many crystal chandeliers, and made our way up the carpeted marble steps. The huge reception room was full. All the children of Budapest must have been there.

Mother took a cursory glance around the room and announced, "None of your friends are here! Let's go home." I knew she hadn't made an attempt to find my friends, but I didn't argue. I had lost my festive mood and didn't really care anymore. So we left and silently retraced our steps to our apartment.

After the holiday, when groups of my classmates congregated at recess to talk about the great time they had at the dance, I moved away.

———

A few years ago, I tried to reconstruct the events of my inheritance and buying Zoli's estate by requesting the records of the public trustee, but very little information was available. Most of it, they claimed, was destroyed. I had enough information to place a claim for compensation in 1991 for the estate. They found the deed and they awarded me bonds based on the size of the building and land, nothing for the animals or the still. These bonds had to be used toward bidding either for my own property or another. There was a market for the bonds, and I authorized a relative to sell them for me. The proceeds came to one thousand American dollars.

Katalin, Eva and Julika, 1951

Christmas Eggs

Post-war Hungary, when I was growing up, was rife with political oppression that permeated every facet of life. Even small children, who could barely understand what this stilted political correctness was all about, sensed things were somehow out of alignment. For instance, the communists officially abolished Christmas and replaced it with the "Festival of the Spruce Tree." This meant that decorated trees were all right, people had the day off from work, but any religious reference was taboo. All forms of religion or reference to religious holidays were banned. People whispered about politics, church and religion, taking care not to be overheard by children who might inadvertently repeat it at an unguarded comment.

In 1948, while I was in grade two, instead of the traditional school Christmas play, "The Sakhalin Visit" was performed, a drama about Lenin visiting that eastern outpost. I had no idea where Sakhalin was or why Lenin went there. I didn't really understand who Lenin was. We were crammed into the large, dingy gym in which a few naked light bulbs burned. The light didn't penetrate from the large windows, because of the brown paper that replaced the shattered glass. I cannot recall much about the play, except for watching in fascination the grade-four girl —it was an all-girls school— who played Lenin, wearing a pointed beard of cotton batting. The beard bobbed up and down as she said her lines fiercely, in the fashion of Lenin, revealing her fresh young face under it from time to time.

Mikulás, the celebration of Saint Nicholas or Santa Claus on December 6th, was considered a secular holiday and was much more fun for us children. To observe this holiday, there was no need for whispers, no subterfuge. We polished our boots the night before and put them in the window for Mikulás to fill with fruit and candy, if we had been good, or with a switch of leafless branches if we had been bad. No one I knew ever got a switch. The only ones I ever saw were in the candy shop window —gold painted ones, decorated with lovely ribbons and covered in candy. When I asked my mother for one of those, she said she couldn't afford anything that fancy. So when I saw a man come out of the shop carrying one of these decorated switches wrapped in tissue paper, I thought he must be a millionaire.

I had no reason to complain about my bounty. Both my boots were always full to the brim and often, a small package of non-edible gifts was beside them. The gifts were usually practical, like new socks and underwear and maybe a book. Later in the day, a number of relatives would drop by with a chocolate bar or a small bag of sour drops for me.

At that age, I was quite oblivious to the fact that money, food and consumer goods were scarce and caused hardship for the adults. I didn't realize butcher shops should sell meat, not just the great slab of lard that graced the center of the counter at the shop nearest to our apartment. The grocery shop carried bread, milk, butter, bologna, and jam in a block. I knew butter was for special occasions only, because it was expensive, and I couldn't miss the salami, sliced ham, sardines and other fine foods about which my grandmother reminisced, since I had never acquired a taste for them.

I wouldn't have missed eggs, either, if the adults hadn't talked about them so much. Eggs were scarce and coveted. If a store got a small flat of eggs, word spread in the neighbourhood like wildfire: "They're distributing eggs at the corner store!" They made it sound as if the shops were giving them away, and it surprised me when my mother paid the clerk. They usually rationed it to one egg per person. Often, the line-up was thirty minutes long, and you never knew whether the supply would last until you got your turn.

My Great-Aunt Anna was a marvellous cook. She was raised in the country on a big estate with numerous servants, and had moved to Budapest many years before to keep house for her brother-in-law when her sister died. He had a lovely apartment in his own six-unit building in the Buda Hills, in the green belt of Budapest. Of course, the building was nationalized with all others, but he remained in his own suite. In summer, Aunt Anna grew vegetables and canned the fruit from the sour cherry and apricot trees in the garden, as well as tended her prized red climbing roses. In my mind's eye, I always see her with her soft and kind face framed by a bunch of fragrant red roses. Mother, Grandmother and I often visited her and Great-Uncle Jóska on Sunday afternoons, when I followed her into her kitchen. Talking to her while she prepared coffee and a tray of treats for her visitors was always a special time for the two of us. Her kitchen was a magic place. The counter was a great marble slab where she concocted wonderful candy, spreading it on the cold marble to cool and shape. I was in awe of the beautiful Delft-blue coffee grinder on her wall and watched her as she decorated the brewed coffee with a dab of apricot meringue to make it look as dramatic as any confectionery shop delicacy downtown.

One Sunday early in December, I caught the adults discussing Aunt Anna in hushed tones: "...We have to do something..." "...she's really depressed..." "... she's too old to understand or to change..." "She lives for her Christmas baking…" —filtered out from the living room. The following week found my mother, who hated line-ups, standing in line for one egg in one store and for another egg in another store. Even my grandmother, who always felt anything to do with the kitchen was beneath her, went in search of eggs and stood in line to get one, carrying her precious egg home in the pocket of her fur coat. Eventually, Mother took all the eggs the extended family could procure to Aunt Anna, so she could bake her usual array of pastry for Christmas.

On Christmas morning, we took the streetcar for the snow-covered hills of Buda, leaving behind the brown muddy slush of Pest. We trudged up the hill from the streetcar to the house in the crunchy snow. In Pest, you never saw much white snow. As soon as it fell, the crowds mashed the glistening white into a brown slushy mess that got your boots dirty. When we got there, Aunt

Anna embraced us in a warm welcome. A few other relatives were there already and I made my rounds for hugs and approval, eventually ending up sharing the big armchair with my Great-Uncle Jóska.

The Christmas tree stood in the dining room. It wasn't very big, but its beauty riveted me. It had a gold star on top, multicoloured metallic glass baubles, white twisted candles in clip-on holders and "angel hair" —glass wool— spread over the whole. The flickering candles played their dance over the ornaments and the snowy white angel hair magnified the effect.

Next to the tree on the table was a huge silver tray that held the most fantastic collection of cookies and pastry I had ever seen. Aunt Anna bustled in with coffee for the adults and a cup of hot chocolate with whipped cream for me. She passed the tray of pastry around and pressured everyone to take more.

When everyone was settled, Anna, statuesque in her traditional embroidered and beaded Hungarian costume, stood beside the grand piano and sang the old Christmas carols, accompanied by her nephew Luli. Her clear soprano rang through the apartment; her face was uplifted, her eyes shining bright. Her happiness radiated like a beacon through the whole apartment — you could almost touch it.

When she finished, the company broke up into smaller groups to converse, more sweets were passed around, the uncles remarked on my growth and the aunts commented on my pretty dress. Luli continued to play well-known jazz pieces of the thirties, winding up with "Old Man River," his voice as deep as he could make it to imitate Paul Robson.

Friends and Neighbours

Being an only child, I spent a lot of time socializing with adults. In the early years, when both our finances and government regulations allowed us to keep a maid, I always had a good companion in the farm girls who kept house for us. They were willing to sing me to sleep with folk songs of the village where they hailed from and talk about country life. I preferred real stories to fairy tales, and they had a ready supply.

The first maid's name and personality, or lack of it, has faded into the foggy past. She was with us for a very short time, right after the war when food was terribly scarce. She bossed my mother around, demanding that she trade more gold for better foodstuffs so she could build me up. I was very skinny and fragile-looking, according to the pictures. Near starvation in the bomb shelter, followed by a bout of whooping cough, had taken its toll. This woman was going to "cure" me if it took bullying my mother. The only thing that remains in my memory is the taste of the spicy honey cake she baked. I've tried every honey cake recipe I've come across and sampled some from the finest bakeries, but none compared to the memory. Perhaps because I haven't experienced that kind of hunger since that period of my life, and the culinary art of this maid was the first real taste sensation for me.

Erzsi, our next maid, was strict but loving. She was my friend. She had the patience of Job when I dawdled in front of store displays, wanting to take in every detail of the wares displayed. Naturally, the toy store windows held the greatest fascination for me, but I was quite happy to look at just about anything, even the milliner's portal. I loved the two florist shops in our neighbourhood. One was a large shop with marble pedestals displaying dignified formal arrangements and sombre funeral wreaths. It always had something exotic and unusual on display, like birds of paradise stalks or potted lilac bushes festooned with artistically rolled crepe paper to hide the pot.

The smaller flower shop across the boulevard catered to a less exacting clientele. People zipped in for small bouquets of carnations to take to a sick friend, or a bunch of roses to a birthday celebration. Their window display would have been ordinary but for the miniature Japanese gardens on display. These were mostly cacti planted in shallow dishes with tiny pebbles to form walks, larger ones to imitate boulders, a strip of mirror was the stream though the landscape, and a little wooden bridge led to the other side of the brook. Sometimes little paper umbrellas, like the ones we get in cocktails, were placed in this landscape and occasionally a tiny porcelain figure of a lady in a kimono or a man carrying a fishing pole finished the little montage. Each scene, no more than eight inches in diameter, was a unique piece of art by itself, allowing my imagination to see that far away, exotic land and perhaps imagine myself in it.

I even stopped at the glazier's shop to admire the various mirrors, especially the paddle- shaped hand mirror made entirely of glass that had a scalloped, burnished edge. I kept visiting that mirror and when I had almost the right amount of money put away to buy it for my mother for her birthday, I asked them to set it aside for me. I guess I caused a bit of a sensation with my "grown up" request, because I later found out that the owner told just about everyone in the neighbourhood how well I negotiated the transaction. Mother loved the mirror and was impressed with my ability to save up such a large sum of money from my meagre allowance.

I loved the stationery store on the corner. The owner, until the store was nationalized, was my friend. I could come and visit any time and "window shop" inside among his display cases. I'm sure part of the attraction was the colourful ceramic entrance frame, created by the well known artist Komlós. I loved to look at the coloured pencils, watercolour paints and erasers on display, and enjoyed the smell of wood shavings that permeated the store from the pencils. I fantasized about how I'd buy a whole set of coloured pencils or a mechanical pen that would change colors when you pushed the appropriate lever on the side and get a real "Elephant Eraser," an expensive brand, the ultimate possession for status at my school, if I came into some unexpected money. As it was, I could only buy one coloured pencil that was blue at one end and red on the other. I also bought my watercolour paints one coin-sized cake at a time and single sheets of the art paper as demanded by my teacher. I looked longingly at the full paint sets and coloured pencil sets a few of my classmates acquired, but most of us couldn't afford such a luxury.

Erzsi was a good companion even when busy. I perched on the kitchen stool while she kneaded the bread, peeled potatoes or polished silver and I asked her a lot of questions. Erzsi always explained what she was doing and why. She was a very accomplished cook and housekeeper, and I guess I learned a lot from her without realizing it at the time. Suddenly, after an argument with Mother about overstepping her powers — borrowing Mother's raincoat— she quit and was replaced by Böbe.

Böbe couldn't have been more than seventeen. She was fun. She went about singing all day and I loved it. She probably wasn't as capable as her predecessor, but she was lively and great company for me. Her eyes always sparkled. Mother called her flirtatious. She was happy to take me to the park to play in the sand box, where she could sit on the bench gossiping with her friends, usually about their boyfriends, while I played. On her days off she dated soldiers, young conscripts from the country, much to my mother's disapproval.

I don't know if it was years or months later and I can't remember the events leading up to it, but Erzsi returned and we continued in our previous routine.

As property was nationalized and tighter and tighter restrictions were brought in to control every aspect of life in keeping with the doctrine of communism, keeping a maid became political suicide as well as a luxury that hardly anyone could afford anymore. Erzsi left us and took a job as a clerk in a nearby government-run grocery store. I visited her in the store often until we left Hungary in 1956. Her eyes always lit up at the sight of me and she always made time to talk to me.

The next occupant of our maid's room was Juci. We inherited her when her former employer emigrated to South America and Juci, who was probably in her sixties then, found herself without a roof over her head. Since the maid's room stood empty, Mother took her in exchange for cleaning our apartment once a week, and found her a full slate of cleaning jobs for the rest of the week. She was loyal and kind, but a constant problem because she drank. Many a Sunday morning Mother had to bail her out from the police station, where she was taken from some seedy bar the night before. She always promised never to do it again, but her promise didn't last long.

Juci was missing several fingers on each hand, the result of some childhood accident, but that didn't keep her from making the best stretched-dough strudels in the world. I can see her nimble figure running around the cloth-covered kitchen table, tugging at the fragile dough, willing it to become paper-thin and transparent before becoming too dry and brittle to manipulate. Juci's loving heart found a way of expressing her emotions through her art of strudel-making, and she used her strudels to heal emotional hurts. Her answer to my grandmother's shop being nationalized, the Kövi's being exiled to the country, or my being quarantined at the height of summer for possible exposure to scarlet fever was strudel. Strudel so delicious that it made you forget your troubles and could sooth your aching heart!

She had to leave when further government regulations made it impossible to keep our two bedroom apartment intact. I was sad to see Juci go. Even as a child, I instinctively knew she needed a "keeper." Mother fulfilled that role while she was with us, taking part of her wages away before she could spend them in the bar and saving them for up for her to buy such necessities as a warm winter coat. Mother arranged for another similar position for Juci —room in exchange for cleaning— with a friend, quite a distance from our place. I don't think she got as close to that family as she did to ours. A few months later, we heard she was found frozen on her mother's grave in the cemetery. Suicide?

Alcohol? We'll never know, but she was definitely a victim of the changing times. She wasn't equipped for independence.

Nearly every evening, Mother and I went for our regular walk on the boulevard. Predictably, the outing started with Mother buying me a small, inexpensive chocolate bar. The walk never changed. It started from our corner heading toward the Danube, crossed the boulevard to the other side, past the Theatre of Comedy and home. On the way, we stopped in several stores to buy bread, milk, cold-cuts and other necessities, all in different stores. Mother stopped to chat with neighbours or friends. Sometimes she ran into people she haven't seen for years and caught up on years of news with them. It was a very busy transportation hub with a lot of foot-traffic. While they talked, I looked at the shop displays. —I loved "our" stretch of the boulevard, the colourful displays in the windows, the crowds of people heading in all directions —some rushing, some sauntering, young and old— going somewhere.

The stores were interesting, too. One store sold household chemicals and cleaning products directly from barrels. The heady smell of mothballs, mixed with that of soft lye soap, dry cleaning fluid and bleach is still in my nostrils when I think about it. Next to it was the pharmacy with its own smells, dominated by that of cough syrup. It, like almost all pharmacies, had a big philodendron growing in its window. I suppose it's meant to be a symbol of health.

The bakery, the famous Glázner's, across the street infused the entire block with the tantalizing aroma of freshly-baked breads and a vast selection of sweet and savoury buns. The theatre was in ruins for most of my childhood, badly damaged by bombs during the war. If I had my tricycle or later, my scooter with me, I'd use its grand curving driveway to ride up and down and imagine myself arriving in a car wearing a ball gown for some important premiere.

Since there were no children my age in our building and Mother didn't allow me to go by myself to the playground where others congregated, I visited people in our six-story building for companionship or roamed around the immediate neighbourhood.

My allowed territory was about four city blocks, where I visited some of the friendly shopkeepers, chatted with neighbours, and stopped into the restaurant to visit with Annus Néni and her staff on the back stoop in the afternoon.

There were tenants I visited regularly. One lady always handed me her cookbook or her baby book to read. I pored over the illustrations in the cookbook, learning the names of the various cuts of meat from the charts. I studied her baby book carefully and applied the knowledge gained to bathe, diaper and dress my dolls. Another of our neighbours supplemented her husband's earnings by doing custom knitting on a semi-manual machine in her living room. When she had a lot of orders, she'd ask me to roll her skeins into balls on a hand-cranked machine. I enjoyed the work, and she showed her appreciation by knitting a sweater for my mother from wool we provided. I was very proud of Mother's new sweater, the fruit of my labour, and never failed to tell everyone about it when she had it on.

My favourite hangout was the bindery run by Mr. Kis. His shop, filled with books in various state of repair during the process of rebinding, always smelled of glue. A stench if you weren't used to it, but because of my pleasant memories, a comfort-odour to me. He was a craftsman. He lovingly took apart the old, yellowed volumes, re-sewed their spine and created a new cover from scratch. I loved to watch when he had a fine binding to do in Moroccan leather. He lined it with paper with a multicoloured ripple pattern, and then I held my breath as he applied the gold foil with a small branding iron, painstakingly creating the title, letter by letter, and a border of delicate design, both on the cover and on the spine. It was obvious he liked this part of his work best. He never hurried, and his whole demeanour was of peace and satisfaction. He caressed the finished volume with loving strokes. As I got older, he gave me small jobs to do, sorting paper or perforating the waste paper to make small notepads. I loved using the perforating machine in the back. Although it was hard to reach the pedal, the bank of needles coming down and punching tiny little holes in the wads of paper at the pressure of my foot was fascinating and my first job satisfaction. In return for the work I did, I got free notebooks and paper for school.

Mr. Kis had two sons, just slightly older than me, and on very hot summer days, he closed early and took them swimming to the Lukács pools. Mother and I bumped into him on one such an occasion. He was appalled to find out that even after many swimming lessons; I still sank more often than I floated. Swimming lessons at the Lukács were always conducted by gruff old men who placed a cold, wet canvas belt around my middle, hooked the belt to a long pole and counted, one, two, three while I tried to move my arms and legs. They walked the length of the pool with me suspended from this pole like a hapless fish, but they never explained, never instructed. Mr. Kis decided to teach me to swim right there and then. With an arm under my sinking body, he explained about breathing, floating and strokes. In two afternoons, he had me swimming the length of the pool. I never became a great swimmer, but I thank Mr. Kis that I can swim at all.

———

I visit the old neighbourhood every time I'm in Budapest. The apartment building has never been fully restored from its war-time wounds, and has had scaffolding around it for decades to protect the passers-by from falling plaster. What a grand place it must have been when my mother and father moved there in 1936! Its former beauty is well hidden in neglect now. I sit in the sidewalk café that was my grandmother's hangout and search the faces for familiar lines, but never actually find anyone I know. Most of the stores have changed, only the upscale florist and the stationery store bear witness to my childhood memories.

The stationery store is still there, complete with the ceramic entrance and smell of wood shavings, but oddly, now that I can afford it, the items on display seem mundane. The entrance decoration by Komlós must be worth a small fortune. Small Komlós ceramic figures have become very collectible and scarce, fetching a high price in the antique shops.

I have an inscription in my treasured autograph book from Erzsi which says: "Even though you often made me angry, I always loved you very much." The funny thing is, I don't recall Erzsi even raising an eyebrow, let alone getting mad at me. I wonder when and how I made her angry. She certainly didn't show it.

Propaganda and Fear

Communist propaganda permeated every aspect of our lives. Every day, we had a flag-raising assembly in school. Several hundred students crammed into the part of the hallway that was a bit wider than the rest, blocking the way to the only functioning bathroom in the building. One of the students or a teacher delivered rousing speeches or poems. Looking back, I wonder if a fire safety inspector would have allowed such a concentration of bodies, but I've never seen any safety inspector in all my school years. The whole assembly was a farce and everyone knew it. Judging from the composition of my class, only about ten percent of the children came from families that could be considered sympathetic to the communists. Of about thirty teachers, judging from their comments in class, only one or two truly supported the system. Yet, we went through the motions of prescribed speeches and songs. There was one particular rousing song that we sang frequently, "...the peace camp cannot be defeated..." The "peace camp" being, in the jargon of the time, the countries on the east side of the Iron Curtain, joined in the common goal of defeating the imperialist capitalists in the west to make communism the international norm. This was supposed to be a very serious part of the assembly. Peace in Hungarian is "béke," but we invariably we sang "béka," which means frog, loud and clear. We thought it was funny. The teachers and the principal pretended to be deaf.

We learned street savvy early; we knew where and when we could get away with such flagrant touting of the rules. At an early age, we learned to be very cautious of what we said outside our homes. There were several taboos. We didn't speak about getting a gift parcel from a relative in the west. In fact, it was dangerous even to have a relative in the west, so we didn't mention that to strangers. My uncle, who lived in Spain, sent parcels whenever he could. It didn't happen often, since Hungary had blacklisted Spain. Even letters had to be sent via a third party who lived in a country that had postal relations both with Spain and Hungary. Hence, we never knew what handwriting or foreign stamp signalled a long-awaited letter from Róbert. Censors often opened the letters both coming and going; therefore, messages were carefully constructed with veiled references to real events. For instance, if we received money from my uncle via the underground black-market, the letter might sound like this: "Grandma is getting better. Yesterday, I bought Eva a doll for five hundred forints. The specialist says her heart is weak, but with rest and medication, she should be fully recovered soon." The meaning of this was that mother got the five hundred forints sent through the underground system yesterday. The references to Grandma's health were true and most likely the bulk of the money was spent on the specialist, since Grandma didn't have health coverage.

The rules for what a parcel from the west could contain were very restrictive. Used clothing was permissible, but the duty extracted from the recipient in Hungary was at the whim of the customs inspector. I was about thirteen when such a parcel arrived. Since it was difficult for my mother to take time off work to clear it through customs, I offered to go to the customs warehouse and see if I could get the parcel cleared. The customs officer, perhaps because he wasn't used to dealing with such a young person, talked with me while he opened the parcel in front of me. My excitement was genuine and he could see it. There was a lovely blue corduroy jacket, a beautiful brown tweed dress and a well-used compass set in a Moroccan leather case for me, along with some smaller items for my mother and grandmother. I frankly told the officer how much this all meant to me. We were in dire straits and couldn't afford clothes for me. That winter I had outgrown nearly everything. He only had to look and see that my sweater was so small, I could hardly move. As to the compass, I loved geometry, but had to borrow a set from a neighbour or a schoolmate every time I had homework. He smiled and set the duty to a ridiculously small amount. Surely, Mother would have had to pay much more; I remember singing to myself all the way home.

The used clothing parcels were infrequent because the mail situation made such a venture very complicated for my uncle. The prepaid parcels were more numerous. He asked a friend in another country to pay at a special bureau dealing with Hungarian export-import, and we got a voucher to shop at the IKKA store, a special shop where these vouchers could be redeemed. After he married, the other country was usually Morocco and the friend was his mother-in-law, a Hungarian émigré in Tangiers. For the size of vouchers my uncle could afford, there were set combinations of food items to choose from, or we could select yardage from the four or five bolts of cloth that were available. I'm sure there were other things too, but Mother nearly always chose the food parcels. These contained a pound or two of coffee, a pound of tea, a pound of cocoa, a few tins of sardines, plus some rice and a bottle of liqueur. The first three items were worth their weight in gold, either for personal use or for resale on the black-market, for there was a huge shortage of those items. Sardines were a special treat because they were rarely available in the stores. We opened the tin with much ceremony. There was fresh bread and butter to receive this delicate gift of the sea, then Mother dissolved a tablet or two of artificial lemon and sprinkled the "lemon juice" over the fish. Real lemons were scarce as well. We always washed the meal down with tea, made by taking a small pinch of leaves and boiling it to death in a saucepan to make sure not one molecule of flavour went to waste. I don't know the reason they always added rice all the food packages. Rice has never been an essential item in the Hungarian diet and was never in short supply. Perhaps there was a glut of rice imported from our Chinese allies, which had to be used up somehow. While we could always use it, we didn't find it very exciting. The liqueur was always Császárkörte, a very sweet pear liqueur that Grandmother loved as a nightcap on winter nights. She took her time drinking the thimbleful she poured into a shot glass, use her tongue to lick out the very last drop, sighing with satisfaction. A bottle lasted her an entire year.

Discussing religion was another taboo subject. Most people quit going to church altogether, for fear of being seen and reported to the authorities. The few who did go often went to a church in a faraway suburb, where they'd be less likely to be observed or recognized. They definitely didn't talk about it. When the convents and monasteries were abruptly closed by the government, many nuns, monks and priests found themselves on the street without a home or the means to support themselves. Devout families took them in and told their neighbours they had distant cousins from the country living with them. I frequented one such home of my friend Katalin to play dolls with her. Everything was so hush-hush about the strange, silent woman I saw there that knew without being told I shouldn't mention having seen her.

Despite all these precautions, there were leaks. At the end of high school, my friend Katalin, who had excellent marks and qualifications, submitted an application to go to a teachers' college. Soon after that, the principal called into her office. That principal was Mrs. Otta, the same woman who some years earlier made me quake with fear. She sternly told Katalin that people as ignorant of the appropriate social path as to go to church on Sundays couldn't be trusted with the education of the future generation. Her submission to teachers' college was therefore denied. Katalin took typing instead. She worked as secretary using her considerable language skills —she was fluent in German and English— to write correspondence about exporting dishtowels and socks.

Adults had it even harder. They had to attend interminable political lectures and meetings at work. I remember passing the Ministry of Mining as I came home from school, and hearing the rhythmic clapping that was expected at every mention of the name Rákosi, the communist head of state in Hungary, Stalin or Lenin ringing out from one of the meeting rooms. The clapping was compulsory. In factories, the speeches extolled the virtues of the great Soviet workers who learned to work faster to build Communism. One of these workers, Stahanov, was particularly venerated for increasing his production, and Hungarian factory employees were persuaded into to emulate him with promises of more pay and a medal they could wear to show their achievement. The problem was that when a few broke the performance "norm," they raised the norm. This increase in fabrication speed resulted in the manufacture of many rejects and in poor quality goods being produced. This also meant fewer or inferior goods in the stores that already suffered from under-stocking.

From time to time, a group of serious-looking people descended on an unsuspecting apartment building and, like modern day proselytizers, knocked on doors to convince the hapless inhabitants of the advantages of communism, which would improve the lot of the average citizen. From time to time, they also sold bonds to "invest" in the future of Hungary to people who could hardly afford food. Unlike the religious callers, these visitors couldn't be turned away with excuses of supper burning or a child needing homework help. They had to be let in. No one dared to refuse. Everyone bought a few bonds.

Because of these ad hoc visits, very few households left expensive decorations like a silver service in view, for fear the visitors would report them for owning luxury items that they most certainly had acquired during the previous regime. This would label them as bourgeois and, by extrapolation, as enemies of the state. Some people went as far as having the works of Lenin and Stalin lying about, or even had a picture of one of them over the sofa to set the proper scene for these unexpected visitors. Hypocrisy? Maybe, but self-preservation was on everyone's mind. If it meant living with the picture of the great leaders as props, so be it.

Being declared an enemy of the state could mean a number of things, from job loss to imprisonment. People so branded were often shunned by their family and friends, who were afraid that even being seen talking to them or visiting with them might get them the same label. Fear was everywhere. The better jobs were closed to those deemed enemies of the system, and their children were often barred from higher education.

My mother painted silk scarves and repaired stockings for a living. She had trouble buying the necessary aniline dyes for the scarves. One day she ran into a widower, Árpád, whom she hadn't seen in years. Árpád's deceased wife was Mother's school chum. They talked and she found out he was a chemist. She told him of her problems with the dyes, and he promised to find out if there were alternatives she could use. He wrote down our telephone number to call if he learned something and on parting, he bought me a small bag of candy in a nearby store. A week later, Árpád called with a suggestion. Mother thanked him for the trouble he took and that was the end.

A couple of years later, Mother was summoned to the central police station for questioning. There was no hint of the reason for asking her to go, and none was expected. Mentally, she went through her life and connections one by one, trying to think of someone that could have reported her for some infraction, but though her imagination became wilder and wilder, there wasn't any obvious reason for the summons. It was a very tense evening as she went through many scenarios. The next day she bade us a tearful goodbye, since people receiving such summons were often never seen again. After a full day of questioning, she returned home exhausted and somewhat relieved, although there was no assurance she wouldn't be summoned again. After hours of interrogation, she had been told that the chemist, Árpád, was arrested for having sex orgies in his home and since Mother's phone number was in his address book, they thought she was one his ladies. At age twelve, even I found this tale less than believable. We never saw Árpád again. The charges could have been drummed up or real.

People disappeared constantly, usually arrested in the middle of the night. It was easy to tell when such an arrest took place in the neighbourhood. The next morning, small groups formed, whispering and looking around for eavesdroppers. As soon as a stranger or a child was within earshot, they'd exclaim about the weather in loud, cheerful tones and then returned to whispering.

Listening to western radio stations was another forbidden activity. Few people had strong enough shortwave receivers to pick them up, so we often had four or five trusted neighbours and friends in our apartment to hear Radio Free Europe and the Voice of America. The radio was tuned low so nosy neighbours could not overhear the broadcast. The government built interference stations to obstruct the sound, which often resulted in loud crackling and whistling that that carried. My stepfather, Zoli always had one hand on the volume knob throughout the program to react instantly when the volume changed.

Having a telephone put us into the elite of the thirty-six-unit apartment building. There were only four telephones in the building. Those who wanted a telephone put in their application showing just cause, then waited for years, sometimes decades, to get a telephone. We were fortunate that our phone request, due to Mother's business needs, was granted before the waiting period became ridiculously long. Emergency calls for other tenants came to our number and I had to deliver messages at all hours. This situation, of course, put me in the position of knowing everyone's business, but as young as I was, I never repeated anything. Everyone in the building, from the children to the very old, was my friend and I knew a careless word could compromise them.

Adults found safe entertainment and free self-expression in spectator sports. Almost everyone was a sports fan. The outstanding performance of Hungarian athletes in several events —especially in swimming— at the Helsinki Summer Olympics spoke to the people's pride. When the athletes arrived back at the Western Railroad Station, a huge crowd greeted them and carried the triumphant team members on their shoulders all the way to their homes, amid cheers from the crowds lining the boulevard. I witnessed one of these impromptu parades where a swimmer was carried to her apartment building in our neighbourhood. It was unforgettable. Everyone felt triumphant, as if to some extent they were winners, too.

Soccer was the national sport and the games were well attended. On Sundays, stadiums were filled to the rafters. The biggest game, England versus Hungary in 1953, lives in everyone's memory as an indelible highlight. Almost everyone remembers where they were on that momentous afternoon. During the game, I was heading home by trolleybus from my friend Marilla's.

Throughout the forty-five minute trip from Zugló, at every stop a clutch of people shouted the results into the bus. Since few people had radios, many put their radios into their open windows so neighbours and passers-by could enjoy the game. The game ended in a score of six to three. David won over Goliath! Hungary beat the mighty English team. Total strangers hugged on the street.

———

In Canada, I revel in the freedom of speech and take interest in politics. I take my responsibility to contribute to democracy, as an informed voter, very seriously. From time to time, I take it so far as to get involved as a volunteer for a candidate.

I still love sardines, but have a terrible habit of hoarding food. My freezer, cupboards and storage in the basement are always full. From time to time, I resolve to use up the surplus, because it's extra work just to maintain it and it makes no sense to have so much when we have two major grocery stores open from eight in the morning until ten at night just ten minutes from our home. Somehow, the shelves and freezer soon fill up again.

Palatinus

Hot summer days remind me of the wonderful summer I spent at the Palatinus. I must have been seven or eight when Mother announced we weren't taking a holiday that year. Instead, we were buying a monthly pass to the Palatinus and would spend every day there. For my mother, this was just one of the early signs of our shrinking financial fortune she bore with gloomy resignation, but to me this declaration was heaven, especially when I found out my best friend Marilla and her family had made the same decision. I adored Marilla. Whenever we got together, we really enjoyed each other's company. When I was at their house, she showed off her gymnastic ability on the rug-beating frame in the yard and I honestly admired her flips, for I wasn't athletic at all. We played with toys or a board game without ever having a disagreement or a quarrel. What made the friendship even more special was that we could see each other only infrequently, because she lived in the far suburb of Zugló and I lived in the inner city.

The Palatinus, affectionately called the Pala, is a set of open-air swimming pools, located in an enclosed park of six acres on Margit Island. At the height of the season, the Pala sees twenty thousand visitors a day. The now-renovated Palatinus is still a favourite place for the people of Budapest. Its amenities and easy access by public transportation from most parts of the city are the sources of its popularity. Margit Island sits in the middle of the Danube, the river that slices through the city, dividing Buda from Pest. It's an incredible 247 acres of green area, reserved for recreational activities, right in the heart of the metropolis.

The walk to the pools was always stimulating. The cool morning air, the bustle of traffic as we walked the six blocks to the bridge, and crossing the bridge to continue in the shade of the ancient majestic trees, was all very exciting and wonderful.

The changing rooms were usually buzzing with activity by the time Mother and I got there at about ten. Those people who could afford it got a little private changing room; when they were ready, they had to call the attendant to lock it up. A little cheaper and a lot noisier were the lockers in a communal room, where people changed at a public bench, then got the attendant to lock up their things in one of the small individual cabinets that lined the walls. This is where we went. Children were everywhere, adding noise to the mothers' queries of "Where is your towel?" and "Did you take the suntan lotion?" echoed through the large room. By the time a mother got her children changed and started to the park, laden with everything she needed for them — including the day's food supply— she must have been exhausted. But not Marilla's mom! She arrived with her two daughters, always late to my mother's chagrin, after traveling an hour by streetcar from her home, cool and composed. She never hurried; she arrived immaculately groomed, with a smile on her face and a brief excuse for her tardiness, always in control of herself and her girls without getting excited.

From the changing rooms, we headed straight for "our spot" to lay out our blankets and claim our small territory. Our spot wasn't far from the changing rooms, a practical consideration in case one of us needed to use the bathroom. Our selected area was on the edge of a grove that gave us gentle shade in the afternoon heat, but was sunny at the beginning of the day, so Marilla's mother could work on her tan. As soon as everyone was settled, we begged to go into the wading pool. There were two wading pools, each the size of a normal community pool. At the deepest part, the water only reached our chest, but —since there were no lifeguards— we weren't allowed to go in by ourselves, thus the great plea commenced to convince one of the mothers into supervising, while the other stayed to guard our stuff. The supervision most often fell to my mother, since Marilla's mom was busy tending to her younger daughter, Roni, a toddler. We stayed in the water for as long as we could, splashing and playing until we ran out of words to plead for five more minutes.

After a few minutes of sitting still, or as still as children can sit on a blanket, Marilla and I left to explore the grounds. We had strict instructions to be back by a given time. It wasn't hard to be punctual, since there was a huge clock fixed to a very tall post in the centre of the compound that was clearly visible from nearly everywhere. Most often, we took the path heading toward the hot pools and then cut across behind the Olympic-size cold pool, where the athletic types were doing laps, then to the open-air gym to watch the breathtaking performances there. Permanent gym equipment —parallel bars, rings, pummel horses and the like— attracted young people —mostly young males— with gymnastic talents. They flipped and swung as if they were alone, but they obviously had one eye on the audience to see if they could attract the admiration of a good-looking girl.

Down a little ways, we watched a game or two of handball played at one of the courts on the sandy ground. Then, we turned and walked slowly past the grand restaurant where formally clad waiters, in white jackets and black bowties, scurried to serve lunch on silver platters to a smattering of affluent clientele. We took great sniffs of the aromas that wafted from the tables, set with starched linen and china. This always reminded us that we were hungry and we picked up our pace, hardly pausing in front of the many little huts that offered fast-food such as sandwiches and snacks. Rounding the two wading pools, we were in sight of our mothers and lunch.

Lunch typically consisted of things that were safe to eat without refrigeration. —Fresh rolls, hard-boiled eggs, cheese and heavily smoked sausages, with fresh tomatoes and the sweet yellow banana peppers that Hungarians love so much, all washed down with cold, unsweetened tea.— We were supposed to rest and sit still after lunch until our food was digested. Most of the time, we played sedate games like cat's-cradle, and listened to the music from the park's scratchy loudspeakers. Each song was paid for by some love-struck admirer, and thus the DJ prefaced it with something like, "To Julia with my undying love —your adoring puppy, Peter."

Occasionally, the music was interrupted with a message

about a lost child or a husband waiting for his wife under the clock. Children darted everywhere; the tricycle vendor peddling ice cream arrived, ringing his bell; the soft drink seller also passed, hawking his chilled soft drinks. We seldom got a treat of ice cream or pop. We knew not to even try to cajole. It simply wasn't in the budget.

Sun tanning at the Pala was an art form. People dedicated themselves to the perfect tan, turning as if on a rotisserie. At the changing rooms, one could pay to be sprayed with suntan oil from head to toe by a woman who held a gun from a compressor and walked slowly around your body. We never got the spray gun treatment, but we were generously basted with Nivea suntan lotion at regular intervals.

The highlight of the day was always the visit to the wave-pool. We anxiously watched the minutes pass on the clock and were well on our way to the other end of the grounds, past the changing rooms, when the siren blew to signal a wave session, sending a ripple of excitement through the entire complex. We splashed, bobbed and shrieked with all the others as wave after wave lifted us off our feet, sometimes breaking over us to make us surface sputtering swallowed water. A wave session lasted about ten minutes and, as a rule, the pool was so full of bodies, we couldn't see the water. After the excitement of the waves, the quiet walk through the rose garden adjacent to the wave-pool was refreshing and the beauty of the large hybrid roses calming.

When we returned to our spot, it was time for the mothers to have their hot pool session. The hot pool was built like a labyrinth of cement partitions formed into benches to sit on and a roof over some of the sections to keep out the sun. The water was chest-high for me, so we held our packages high out of the water to get to a seat and deposit our stuff on the low dividing wall between the benches. The mothers got down to serious gossiping with their regular partners. The water was shallow, and we children roamed around the maze freely in the warm water.

As much as people were strapped financially, the Pala was in its own way a place to show off. Both men and women were decked out with their finest gold chains and the best in bathing attire. Mother had a new bathing suit custom-made of a thick canvas-like material in a floral print of white on dark brown. Since the material had no stretch and zippers were too expensive, a row of small white buttons held it together in the back. She was very proud of her new acquisition, until she had her first hot pool session. As she sat, one by one the buttons started popping, their bridges dissolved in the hot water. She whispered her predicament to me and we quickly made it to the changing rooms, with me holding her together and marching right behind her. Never for a minute did she lose her cool. She walked the long path to the building with her head held high and a forced smile on her face. It turned out that the buttons were made with a new experimental process of turning the waste casein of dairy farms into marketable items. Great innovation, but no one thought to make sure the glue used to make the composite was waterproof.

All too soon, it was time to get dressed and head home. From time to time, if we got out early, we walked in the formal gardens across the road from the Pala with Marilla and her family. This carefully laid-out garden had a large variety roses planted all around its edge, with benches to capture the fragrance and a large formal, bed of annuals in the centre. Tall red cannas, yellow snapdragons, flaming salvias, petunias of every colour, marigolds and delicate asters created a riot of colour surrounded by a lawn and its "Keep off the grass" sign. It was a beautiful place, although rather boring, because we had to stay on the formal paths. There was a stern groundskeeper to make sure everyone obeyed. The walk along the island's shaded and less restricted paths was more enjoyable. Sometimes I convinced Mother to let me go on the swings or climb on a large-branched tree. She was overprotective, and worried constantly that I'd hurt myself. I enjoyed crossing the Margit Bridge and looking at the traffic on the river. Great barges of coal pulled behind small tugboats, excursion ships with holidaymakers revelling to the music of the loudspeakers, little ferries crossing from one side of the river to the other, and kayaks with bronzed oarsmen all held an attraction for me.

Reaching the Pest side of the bridge, my legs seemed to turn to lead. Pest, with its tall brick apartment buildings, stored the heat of the day and like a fire-breathing dragon, spewed the heat back at the pedestrians making their way home. Even the pavement radiated this heat, sapping the energy out of my body. After my favourite summer supper of ice-cold buttermilk, fresh bread and butter with radishes and green onions, I went to bed to dream of the next day at the Pala.

Eva in full young pioneer uniform 1950

The Walls Have Ears

I heard that expression so many times from the adults around me that I even looked for those "ears." Of course, they referred to their paranoid fear of the room being bugged. For instance, a gas inspector from the city would come or the telephone company would send someone to examine the line. Although such a stranger was never left alone for a second while doing his job, immediately after, a thorough search of the apartment was made for listening devices. Everyone was sure that at some point, someone would manage to plant a bug in their homes in spite of the vigilant supervision of any stranger who entered.

Since so many innocent and seemingly ordinary people got into trouble daily on hard-to-believe charges as a result of someone informing on them, this paranoia was understandable. The informants came from all walks of life. In our apartment building, "the vice," the assistant-superintendent, was the first suspect. This big-boned vocal Amazon collected the garbage every evening from the wooden boxes in front of our apartments and occasionally —as seldom as she could get away with it— mopped the stairs and passageways with a dirty rag wrapped around a bald push broom. She could listen at every door on her rounds without raising suspicion and have a close look at everyone's garbage as she collected it. "The vice" knew her power and bossed the tenants with an iron fist. She wouldn't allow criticism of her cleaning job; she said she was now "enlightened to the plight of her working class" and wouldn't allow the parasitic capitalists of the building to oppress her any longer. Retired judges, a practicing heart specialist, former bankers and my mother quaked in fear and handed out insincere compliments to appease her wrath.

In contrast, the superintendent and his wife were sincerely loved, trusted and respected by all. Everyone called him Tati, an affectionate diminutive for father, and his wife was every child's beloved Mami.

Tati's job was to maintain the building in good repair. He fixed locks and leaky plumbing, kept the rickety elevator going without replacement parts, and kept the furnaces stoked with coal and functioning for heating and hot water. That last job was greater than even his ingenuity. The furnaces were constantly broken and most of the time lay in pieces in the courtyard, waiting for the district repairman, because the building was now city property. The leaks in the massive cast iron manifold were beyond Tati's ability to repair. There were two theories for the frequent leaks. One was that the explosion that levelled the hospital in the next block during the Allied raids had shaken the furnace so that hairline cracks formed, which leaked under the pressure of the water. No sooner had they fixed one leak then a new one started. This was plausible, because the explosion must have been massive. I passed the block-size crater, two stories deep, where I was told the hospital once was for years until a new building to house army officers was built in its stead.

The other reason for the leaks was a rumour spread by some of the nastier tenants: was Tati, having drunk heavily while in the pub across the street, forgot to tend the furnace. When he remembered to check the boiler, he found the water was low, turned it on and the cold water hitting the hot furnace caused the cracks. I'm not sure this is even plausible with that kind of furnace. This accusation was whispered with such conviction that I believed it, and grieved for the reputation of my Tati. True, he was an alcoholic, but he was also one of my best friends.

I sat for hours in his tiny workshop, which held an old chair, a shelf cum work bench, and the stool I used when visiting. The ceiling was low and sloped. This cubby-hole was meant to be a porter's office under the main staircase of the building. Tati was a jack-of-all-trades. I watched him as he tinkered with repairing a lock, a small motor, a lamp, a broken clock, a doorbell, or creating some a new gizmo from the many bits of scrap he'd saved. He always explained how the mechanisms worked and I soaked it up. I could watch him fix something with the bits and pieces he had in his cluttered workspace and never get bored. If I questioned him, he explained patiently. I could tell him my childish thoughts. He never laughed at me and always seemed to be interested. Mother couldn't understand how I could spend so much time in Tati's workshop and often asked,: "What can you talk about with that old drunk for hours?" I don't remember her ever waiting to hear my answer about the magic that happened in front of my eyes there. She never understood how fascinating it was to see him make something broken useful again, and how interesting it was to hear Tati explain the way things worked.

I also visited Mami, Tati's wife, an energetic elf who was always cheerful. She was a small, sharp-nosed little woman with thinning grey hair pinned firmly to her nape. She would have been severe looking if not for the constant twinkle in her blue eyes. She loved all the tenants, especially the children. Mami called all the children her own who were born to families in the apartment building since her tenure in 1935, and took great pride in their accomplishments. We all loved and respected her.

Her job was to operate the elevator for visitors when the elevator worked, which wasn't very often because the poor old thing suffered from the maladies of age and lack of proper parts to fix it. She also locked the front door of the building at ten o'clock and opened it again at six in the morning. People returning late from the theatre or concert had to ring her to open the door and tip her for her troubles. In between her chores, she was found in her tiny kitchen, cooking. I spent many pleasant hours watching her, with her cat Cili purring in my lap, and it was here that I learned soap making. She made her own laundry soap from waste fat obtained from the restaurant below and lye, heating it in a large pot. She stirred it like a witch's brew with a large paddle, her form enveloped in the acrid smell of cooking soap. At other times, her nimble fingers moved to insert bits of garlic and bacon into a chunk of meat in preparation for a roast. She worked and chatted, replacing a runaway pin in her bun and tossing waste bits to Fritzi, her other placid fat cat that always lounged on the windowsill.

Mami talked about the old times, the personal history of the tenants, and she talked about my father in glowing terms, for she loved him and respected him. This was very important to me. I was three when I lost my father, and didn't remember him well. I hung on Mami's volunteered tales attentively. Occasionally, a pot boiled over when she was deep in her thoughts and she broke into exclamations in her native Schwabisch German. She never swore, but made up ridiculous sentences to express her displeasure. "Mein Gott! Sechs kinder und kein brot!" (My God! Six children and no bread!) was one of her favourites.

In the evenings, she often showed up to visit with my mother, my stepfather and my grandmother when they listened to the forbidden "Voice of America" or "Radio Free Europe." Mami brought her footstool from home and squatted in the corner listening. No one worried about her informing on them. Mami never told. She never repeated a confidence.

As I got older and started to teach myself cooking, I often took my problems over to her, pot and all, so she could examine it and suggest how I could salvage the mishap. Mami always made her suggestions in a kind tone and ended the discussion with some positive words for my effort. I don't think I'd have continued trying without her help and encouragement.

———

When in 1970 I first returned to Hungary and the apartment building with my two-year-old son, Mami, who was retired by then and had moved to a distant location in the city, got wind of the fact that we were in the building and came, panting, to see us. She laid claim to my son, Leslie, as hers by her standard of heritage, since I too was hers, having been born in her building.

They say children are like sponges, absorbing knowledge without even realizing it. The sessions with Tati probably built a firm base for the technical abilities I developed later. I love to fix things and create gizmos from scrap, a rather unusual talent for a woman of my generation. These abilities stood me in good stead in my working years and earned me a great deal of respect, for I have the courage to tackle any small repair in my home.

Reporting the Enemies

The communists unilaterally declared that the former ruling class had exploited the workers, so therefore the entire class was untrustworthy and just waiting in the wings to create trouble in order to regain its former power. All must be vigilant and weary of these enemies of the people. Aristocrats, the titled elite and former landowners were at the top of this heap of generalization, closely followed by a group referred to as the bourgeoisie, which included bankers and successful merchants as well as intellectuals. The professionals, such as lawyers and doctors, were suspect since they had the money in the former regime to get an education. This later group, called the "intelligentsia," was treated slightly better, albeit with distrust, for their skills were needed to build the communist social order. Eventually, the distrust encompassed even the mom-and-pop storekeepers who made a marginal living. Only the proletariat, the labourers, and the landless farmers, referred to as káder, were to be trusted, because these underdogs of the former regime were to constitute the new elite of society. Artists, writers and actors had to slant their craft to praise communist values, the party, and of course, "the glorious Soviet Union." This led to some hilarious plays, songs and works of art.

The effective turning of society upside down had some humorous and at the same time sad consequences. Society women drove tractors and cleaned offices, while illiterate or nearly illiterate farm workers found themselves in the city, trying to run factories. There was no point in grumbling for either side. It was safer to adapt and try to fit in, repeat the slogans of Marx, Engels or Lenin, or better yet those of Stalin and his Hungarian counterpart, Rákosi, since the last two were still alive and in power.

Rumours were perpetuated by the government propaganda machine of kuláks —well-to-do farmers— hoarding food in the country and being found with large caches of hidden food, trying to sabotage the distribution efforts of the regime, but the people whispered among themselves that all of Hungary's food production went to Russia and we only got the dregs. In Party language, kulák meant 'reactionary.' Expressions like that were used frequently by the media and by the principal at school assemblies. We were to abhor these people who were supposedly parasites of the state, preying on the working class to create dissidence in aid of the imperialist west. They urged us to report them to the authorities. Severe punishment of the delinquent person, usually labour camp, without evidence or a proper trial, followed such a reporting. The law could be twisted to disenfranchise anyone who, they thought, could possibly harm the regime.

The terror was total. People reported neighbours, friends and family for being bourgeoisie, for hoarding goods or having made anti-regime statements, including jokes about the Communist Party, Stalin or Rákosi. This constant threat of reporting, of course, brought out the worst in those whose envy was unbound.

Many used the threat of denouncing someone to the party as a form of blackmail. People were so afraid of being unjustly accused that they didn't object if a friend or neighbour encroached on their property or failed to repay a debt. Sometimes rebellious teenagers reported their parents. You couldn't trust anyone, and the constant fear made people testy. Nasty arguments erupted into major battles over something simple such as a push in a crowded bus or not standing in line, while the crowd took sides and hurled expletives.

The same was true in school. A proletarian child could demand the good pen that a bourgeois child may have gotten from a parcel sent by a relative living in the west and the child would give it up, fearing that the family would face persecution for being a reactionary and an enemy of the state if reported. The school bullies didn't have to use their fists in the schoolyard to get what they coveted. The teachers couldn't intercede, because the proletarian child could denounce them, too. Everyone functioned as a puppet held by invisible strings in a well-choreographed show of spies, envious acquaintances and unsuspected enemies, encouraged by the consequences that the regime meted out. Even in grade five, the children were well aware of which teachers were true communists, and which were vulnerable, due to their background, but we never voiced our knowledge.

Teachers feared to reprimand or give poor marks to the káder children, for they knew how to manipulate the system. They could report the teacher. In extreme cases, the teacher was suspended, sometimes even imprisoned and his career was destroyed. I heard of a case where a high school student who failed his language and literature course, for very poor spelling and composition skills, reported the popular Hungarian language teacher for being a bourgeois. The teacher was summarily dismissed, leaving him and his family destitute. His peers, while shocked and sympathetic, were afraid to lift a finger in his defence, because they too could be next. Since it was against the law to be unemployed, the dismissed teacher desperately had to look for some kind of employment. Often in an episode such as this, friends gave him wide berth for fear of being tainted with his problems. Employers were afraid to hire him due to the same fear. Consequently, in addition to his problems of survival, a person like that, and his whole family, was treated like a leper. When they eventually found a job, it was for low wages as a common labourer in some factory or on a construction site. If they were lucky, there were more hard-luck educated employees in the brigade and they could recite poetry or talk about books during their breaks, but more often, the workmates turned out to be illiterate labourers who looked with suspicion at the soft gentleman in their midst.

A few were lucky, like a family friend, a former gynaecologist, who was fortunate enough to find a job as a purchaser for a construction firm, trudging through the city day after day to find hinges and screws for his company's projects. At least it was a clean job and in the city. In the evenings, he moonlighted, quite illegally, giving private medical services, such as administering injections, to trusted friends. That's how we met him. A specialist prescribed a course of sulpha drugs for me to take intramuscularly. Since getting a regular doctor to give the shots would have been far too expensive, Mother cast around for an alternative and through a friend of a friend, heard about the former gynaecologist. He came twice a week to stab me.

To minimize the danger of being an outsider, all of my classmates, regardless of conviction, enrolled in the Young Pioneer Movement in grade two. We wore first our blue neck-kerchiefs to school, then I think in grade five, we got our red kerchiefs, which signified a higher level, much like going from cubs to scouts. We went to meetings and participated in the compulsory parades on state holidays, singing the many prescribed songs in praise of Lenin, Stalin and, Rákosi.

People bent the truth. We had to write autobiographies at every turn. For instance, I emphasized that my father came from a poor family, had to quit school to support his widowed mother and worked in a factory. I casually mentioned that later he had an auto-parts business, but neglected the word wholesale and certainly didn't brag about his success, fame and being one of the biggest firms of its kind in Budapest. I also forgot to mention that he dabbled in used car sales as well and was an agent for Goodyear, Dunlop and many other international firms. What I wrote was true, just slanted to my advantage. Friends answered as briefly as possible if asked about how their families made their living before the war, and had extremely vague recollections of prewar activities. It was a mass conspiracy. Unimportant people got away with bending the truth.

However, the danger was real for the high profile officials of the government, the former members of other parties and the top echelon of the prewar elite, such as titled nobles, former officials and very rich people. Little people, who didn't have ambitions to become important in any of the regimes and kept their opinion to themselves, did all right. They learned the rules, used them to their own advantage and kept their noses clean. They clapped for Rákosi, wore nondescript clothes, agreed with the party rep in the office and complained only to trusted friends and family. By doing this, they were assured of job security, sometimes a privileged upgraded holiday, summer camp and higher education for their kids. They didn't want to climb higher in the system for bigger status, because it would have posed other dangers. They were little grey mice, unimportant and melting into the background.

Apathetic daze is where I escaped to be safe. A few courageous and rebellious classmates who got into trouble served as a good example for what not to say. I chose to keep quiet, observe, and store information. One would think I would create a world of make-believe, but I never did. I was more of a realist than most of my peers. I hated fairy tales. I preferred to listen to my grandmother talk of the "good old days." Nearly all the books I read had to have a realistic cast of characters. I played with dolls, but they went to the market, got dressed and went to school; mundane things, seldom a flight of fancy.

We kept away from controversy. Mother was the volunteer tenants' representative for the apartment building and a member of the MNDSz, the Women's Democratic League, and later the member of the union in the cooperative where she worked, but not a party member. She did those things that were expected of her in order to keep her home occupation licence and hold her position in the cooperative. Most people set their values aside and worked within the system to fit in and avoid becoming a target.

The regime strongly encouraged "társadalmi munka," which, loosely translated, means "volunteer work," but really meant work without pay to build the socialist society. The words socialist and communist were used interchangeably, possibly to ease acceptance of some of these dictates. My mother volunteered to be the tenants' representative, since this job was the least political. It meant negotiating about cleaning complaints with the vice-superintendent, a tough káder who flaunted her newly acquired rights, thereby keeping her work to a minimum. It also meant keeping track of who lived in the building, and signing papers to show residency or de-registration when a tenant left. Mother conducted tenant meetings, which were mini-wars. Every tenant had a problem, from leaky faucets to broken elevator. The furnace hardly ever worked, and when it broke down, she would be delegated to go to see the officials again to beg for the repair of it.

———

Káder is translated as cadre in my Hungarian-English dictionary. The definition of cadre is a nucleus of trained personnel around which a larger organization can be built and trained or a small, unified group organized to instruct or lead a larger group. In order to facilitate such an elite organization, they arbitrarily divided society into categories, turning the social order upside down; categorizing children by what their parents did for a living before the war.

All the children had the same admonitions from home of "Never tell private family things to your friends or teachers or we can all get into trouble!" and most of us respected that. This is probably the reason that to this day, I never pry. I accept what people want to tell me voluntarily, but never ask questions that could be embarrassing. It isn't that I'm not interested, but I simply can't bring myself to ask because to respect other people's privacy is so ingrained in me. For the same reason, I never gossip. I learned back then that a grain of truth can be twisted to the point where black becomes white and vice versa, and there is no defence.

The people who had higher ambitions to climb to better positions in the system learned to live the lie so perfectly, they no longer separated facts from fiction. They almost believed the lies in their autobiographies and learned to spew the party line so efficiently that they never made a mistake. They had no room for individual thought. They never tripped up because they never allowed themselves the opportunity to disagree with the status quo. They weren't true Communists, but wanted to ensure privileges for themselves. These people are the ones who are suffering the most now. The security is gone, the upgraded pension and hospital care that was to be their reward for supporting the system is almost gone, and people look at them with suspicion, asking, "How could they have survived the previous regime and prospered in it so well if they weren't Communists?" The answer is they had a communist façade, but they were never really believers, just opportunists who followed the rules.

Summers

Mariska was my mother's best friend. Her philosophy was that when you're destitute, you must look for anything —even a blade of grass would do— and pull yourself out of the quagmire. I think that while Mariska hung onto the blade of grass, my mother hung onto Mariska in the hopes of being pulled up with her. Mariska's husband was a family doctor in Soroksár, a rural suburb of Budapest. He worked hard and earned a decent wage in comparison with most people, but it was still difficult to make ends meet, even though his patients occasionally sent him a chicken or a basket of fruit in gratitude. So, Mariska had to help.

They had a house with a relatively big garden, about double the size of a normal single family city lot, where she raised a pig from the waste of her household, a few chickens and one or two geese. We dried our stale bread, saved it all year and took it to Soroksár to feed the pig. In return, they gave us some sausages once they killed the pig. Mariska planted her garden with all manner of berries and vegetables and canned them for the winter. This kind of hard work wasn't in her upbringing and class, but she cheerfully rolled up her sleeves and did it. One day when we came to visit, we found her by the back shed, sitting on a low stool with a fat goose between her legs, her left hand firmly clutching its throat and stuffing corn mush into its beak, as was the custom to fatten geese. My mother, not to mention my grandmother, would have been mortified to be caught in that position, but Mariska just laughed. She was always in great humour.

Mariska had the idea that she could make money painting handkerchiefs and aprons to sell. She converted a large room in her home to a workshop and started her business. Mother joined her, sometimes painting at home and at other times going for a working bee to Soroksár. Later, they branched out to hand-painting silk scarves, which was faster than the painstaking work on cotton and much more profitable. Their relationship was harmonious. While they both did the actual work, each focused on the part of the operation that best suited her talents. Mariska was the decisive business manager, and my mother supplied the artistic imagination in this endeavour. Mother enjoyed the creativity and happily left all business responsibilities to Mariska, who carried off the organizing in great good humour. Sometimes, I went with Mother to Soroksár for a day or two when they had a working bee to satisfy a larger order. While there, I played with Mariska's much younger daughter, Jutka, made her doll's clothes or, when I got tired of Jutka, dug through their library for reading material. This was where I found Charles Lamb's Tales of Shakespeare, which I devoured, then followed it up by reading several plays of the great bard. Starting in grade six or seven, I made it a point to see as many plays of Shakespeare in the live theatres of Budapest as I could. We could get tickets through the school, either free or at a reasonable cost, allowing us to round out our education with live theatre productions of the classics in the curriculum.

When I was about twelve, Mother spent most of the summer commuting and often staying over for several days in Soroksár where, with her friend Mariska and sometimes one or two others would have a marathon scarf-painting session. While the work was hard, they had a lot of fun laughing and joking to break the monotony of painting.

Often, I stayed home with my grandmother and we went for walks, read and discussed books. I had her all to myself, except for the hour or two in the afternoon when she met her friends in the confectionery shop to sip an espresso coffee and chat. I don't know what they talked about, because after saying a polite hello to the old ladies, I was allowed to walk the körút by myself, window shop and enjoy the hustle and bustle of this great boulevard. I loved it and dutifully checked back with my grandmother every fifteen minutes. or so. When she was nearly ready to go home, sometimes she bought me an ice cream cone.

I was quite content with my life, but Mother decided I

should get some fresh air instead of spending the whole summer in what she called "the asphalt and brick jungle." Granted, there wasn't much air and greenery about unless Grandmother and I decided go on a day's outing to Margit Island. To save the bus fare, we walked across the bridge and then strolled under the ancient chestnut trees, discussing the latest books we read, admiring the formal flower beds or pausing at the collection of statues of famous writers, poets and composers. We stopped to rest on one of the benches. Often it wasn't easy to find a bench. Near the playgrounds, mothers with kids occupied them; in more remote corners, lovers or students busily studying took up the space. To return, sometimes we took the little ferry across the narrow branch of the Danube to the embankment and walked along the river to the körút. Back to the clanging of the streetcars, the rush of commuters heading in all directions and the heat trapped in the narrow streets.

Every year, to get me out of the city for at least a short time, Mother found some place in the Buda Hills to send me for at least two weeks of the summer break. For two years, I went to a private villa in Hüvösvölgy, a distant suburb in the hills, where the owner took in children for the summer to augment her husband's earnings and defray the cost of keeping a big house. Big in Hungarian terms of the day, but not much more than about nine hundred square feet in reality. They usually had eight to ten children, ranging in age from three to fourteen. They had a great unkempt garden that stretched for what seemed like miles; it had nooks and crannies to hide in and explore. Tall grasses and wildflowers created a fertile landscape for meditation and thinking. Because most of the kids were much younger than me, at twelve, I was too old and too introspective to spend much time playing. Every excursion into this jungle was a fresh and new experience. I picked wildflowers to arrange in attractive bouquets to take back to the house, where it was appreciatively placed in a glass vase for the dinner table by the kind elderly lady who helped the owner with taking care of the children. As one of the older children, I often helped with the younger ones, played with them and kept an eye out for mischief that would endanger their safety. My favourite

84

was Katika, a four-year-old doll with masses of brown curls framing her pretty face, a warm personality and a cuddly disposition.

The second year, I was pleased to find Katika there when I arrived with one of my friends, a classmate, another Kati. Katika was pleased too, which she expressed with choking-tight hugs and kisses wherever she could reach my face. Kati and I got a very small room, or rather a glassed-in veranda, to ourselves since we were almost grown up and didn't take naps in the afternoons. We could read sitting on our beds or talk in whispers during the quiet hour. Being teenagers, we had a lot to whisper about. We were just developing and found the new shape of our bodies and its functions a fascinating topic. One afternoon, Katika refused to sleep and I agreed to keep her on my bed and read to her so she wouldn't disturb the others. She was cuddlier than usual as we sat together in the corner of my bed reading.

The next morning, Katika and two other children woke with a high temperature. They were diagnosed a few hours later with scarlet fever. The doctor sent everyone home immediately. I was under quarantine —in accordance with the public health regulations— for six weeks for being exposed, but never developed any symptoms of the disease. I was back in the "asphalt and brick" jungle and couldn't even visit with my friends because of the quarantine.

Shortly after, Kati, always frail-looking, was diagnosed with tuberculosis and was sent to a clinic that specialized in its treatment in the Buda Hills. I visited her as often as I could until she was cured and released.

The following year, Mother found me a place in Sas Hegy, where the owner took in only one girl, namely me, as company for her daughter as much as for the money. The idea was good, but in reality, the girl was close friends with a neighbour girl and they left me out of their confidences, which mostly centered on chasing boys. I was bored, outcast and very unhappy. I wrote a letter to my mother, explaining how miserable I was and promising to be good and not get in her way if she would let me come home. Back in the apartment, I kept my word and decided to make myself boys. I was bored, outcast and very unhappy. I wrote a letter to my mother, explaining how miserable I was and promising to be good and not get in her way if she would let me come home. Back in the apartment, I kept my word and decided to make myself useful by doing all the grocery shopping and cooking. I taught myself how to cook and had great fun going to the market and haggling with the sellers for the goods I wanted to buy. The sellers were very kind, because they found such a young girl being a responsible shopper amusing and with great giggles, always gave me a little extra.

I never went on a holiday in the country again.

———

That was the last I saw of Katika, until Vienna in 1956. Mother and I were having a meal in a basement café opened especially to cater to the hordes of Hungarian refugees, when suddenly I was enveloped in the arms of a gangly young girl with masses of brown curls. We talked for while and she told me they were heading to France, where her father had relatives. Her mother watched the little scene from a couple of tables away, then came to investigate the reason her daughter was spending so much time at a stranger's table. When her mother asked, Katika spun around with hands on her hips and said in a scolding tone, "Mother, can't you recognize Kuksi?" Kuksi was a nickname she used for me. She was so sweet, and there was such a lot of love and attachment in those words. I've savoured that memory ever since. That's the last time I saw her. I've attempted to locate her since, but without success.

My friend Kati became a professional concert violinist and we still see each other occasionally and reminisce when I visit Budapest. We usually meet in the café on the körút, where my grandmother used to sit on the terrace with her cronies long ago.

School

Teachers

My school years are a major fog in my ordinarily excellent memory. I was very aware of life around me until I got to grade one, when a curtain descended on parts of my life that wouldn't part until grade seven or eight. I've been trying to part the curtain for several years, but only bits of real light come through the chinks. The full view continues to elude me. It's not clear what caused this memory block: whether it was the pressures of the secretive society that emerged after the Communist party took power, fear of school, or my own ambiguous family life. I suspect a combination of all these made me block out certain details, while they amplified some of the more dramatic events. I simply spent my time in a daze, escaping reality.

I started grade one in 1947, on my sixth birthday in Józsa Néni's private school on Bajcsi Zsilinsky Boulevard. The school was grades one to four in two big rooms of an apartment in a residential building. Grades one and two were in one room, and Józsa Néni alternated between teaching the two grades. Another teacher did the same in grades three and four. I remember little about Józsa Néni; the thought of her elicits no emotion from my subconscious. She was bland and I was neither happy nor unhappy there, just a little bit lost. Józsa Néni didn't make it clear what she expected me to do. The trips to and from school were much more memorable.

I loved to walk past the "Haas and Czjzek" store with its glittering display of fine china and crystal, I loved the musty, friendly smell emanating from the used bookstores, and, near the railroad station, the crowds pouring from all directions into Marx Square were positively fascinating. Peasant women in traditional "many-skirted" outfits had huge baskets strapped to their backs.

They carried produce to the markets in the morning, but now in the afternoon, the baskets were empty and the women headed to the stores of Szent István Körút to spend their earnings on fabrics, notions and shoes, while the men went to the seed store to buy tools, seeds and pesticides for their small plots of land. Our maid, Erzsi, coquettishly flirted with the young soldiers on furlough coming from the railroad station, while holding my hand protectively.

A few days before grade two was to start, my mother told me all private schools had been "nationalized" and I would now be enrolled in the girls' wing of the Szemere Street Public Elementary. Since I had no particular attachment to Józsa Néni, the change left me untouched. Only after entering the new school did its negative aspects dawn on me. The school was a largely un-repaired four-story war-damaged building. The uncivilized conditions of the broken, filthy, unheated toilets with the stinking, always flooded floors inflicted physical pain, because whenever possible I tried to avoid them. Holding your "business" from eight in the morning until one in the afternoon wasn't easy for a seven year old. The papered-over windows kept us in perpetual dimness, while the bulky outline of Vali Néni, our teacher, droned on the dais. The teaching method required reading the same passage over and over again. I suspect those who got more and more fluent in reading this way actually memorized the passages. Between reading out loud in a chorus and copying work from the blackboard, we sat quietly as expected with our hands clasped behind our backs while the teacher explained something. We were sitting on hard wooden plank seats attached to twin desks arranged in three columns and seven rows. This method of learning bored me so much that I switched off. I was accused of daydreaming, but no amount of threats or incentives could draw me out of my exile.

My classmates were more interesting and I listened keenly to their chitchat at recess. We were a truly odd lot. The class was created from the pupils made school-less by "nationalization," a big word that took us years to fully understand. That summer, by edict of the communist government, all private and parochial schools were closed. Most of my classmates came from the respected private school founded and operated by the Anglican sisters, Angol Kissasszonyok. Their backgrounds were all suspicious to the new system. Children of bankers, lawyers, judges, doctors, industrialists, merchants, the bourgeoisie, and a few from aristocratic or semi-aristocratic background made up our classroom. Three or four girls in our class of thirty-two were from the proletariat, or working class, and were automatically considered "spicli" or communist informants. We cultivated their friendship so as not to offend them, but we didn't trust them. We carefully avoided talking about social status, home life, politics, religion, and many other subjects we didn't understand, but were cautioned at home never to broach. Not that we wanted to discuss those things. We were normal, lively, chattering and gossiping girls. After school, we walked home in groups, continuing the chitchat started at recess.

Our teachers, by and large, weren't adherents of the communist doctrine any more than the pupils. They were busy trying to pour some knowledge into our heads and to keep their noses clean. When we altered the words of the communist youth song to mock it, they pretended to be deaf. Yet, true to the strict disciplinary traditions of education in Hungary, we got hauled over the coals for an inappropriate smile, a whisper or other minor infractions during class.

The Hungarian school system, modeled on the severity of German-style discipline, demanded strict obedience to the teacher. We called our teachers by their first names with the designation of aunt, néni, or uncle, bácsi, added to denote respect. While all forms of corporal punishment were abolished years before I started school, verbal abuse was rampant. A teacher could destroy the self-esteem of any child with a cutting remark and ridicule. Coming from the omnipotent teacher, these words carried weight beyond measure and soon spread in the children's community like wild fire, branding the person and his or her psyche for life.

In grade two, my kindly teacher Vali Néni, complained to my mother about my daydreaming. At her suggestion, I was professionally tested for a possible learning disability. The diagnosis was that I suffered from boredom. That was true. I would enjoy reading a story for the first time, maybe even for the second time, but repetition bored me and soon I wandered off into a more interesting world of my own, watching the dust particles dance in the shafts of light that penetrated our gloomy classroom. Vali Néni understood after the test result came back and didn't pressure me. The next year, no one thought of explaining my problem to Olga Néni my third grade teacher. One day when I was off in my world, she made fun of me. She called me Sleeping Beauty, to the hilarity of the class. Her tone made it clear it was meant to be a put-down, indicating I wasn't applying myself to the schoolwork as I should. It took me years to wash off that label and the accompanying smirks among my peers. The scar has faded, but it's never quite healed. I disliked Olga Néni, but I was too afraid to voice it. She was a poor teacher and immensely boring. I was having health problems, complications of rheumatic fever, and was absent a lot. She did nothing to help me catch up. Today, I wonder how many of my health problems were real and how much was due to not wanting to go to school and endure her ridicule? She got her just desserts when she almost caused a revolution among the parents. In teaching long division, she "forgot" to teach us about carrying the remainder and all our work was wrong for weeks, before one of the mothers noticed. They then complained to the principal, and she was severely reprimanded.

A breath of fresh air came in grade four in the person of Juliska Néni. She was very severe, strict, but fair. Her only goal was to teach us as much as she could. We respected her and worked hard, but her severity kept us at a distance. I didn't particularly like her, she wasn't friendly or warm, but I respected her and never complained about the mountains of homework she assigned.

Her severity was a front, as I later found out. In the customary graduating ceremony at the end of grade eight, we strolled through each classroom singing a traditional song of farewell as the pupils of the class stood at attention with their homeroom teachers. When we entered Juliska Néni's classroom, she dissolved into tears. We had been her first teaching assignment, and her severity was a cover for her inexperience. There we were, her first flock ready fly out of the nest into the world, and she became emotional.

My relationship with my other teachers was from was fair to good. I loved geography although Kato Néni, the teacher, was a dour old maid, severe and demanding, who in retrospect conveyed an enormous amount of knowledge in the limited time allotted to her lessons. She succeeded in teaching us so much about the world, its people and customs, that when I read the daily news, I still dip into that knowledge she had us store away.

In grade eight, we had a very tough and demanding physics teacher, Anni Néni. She had a blood-chilling manner and had us quaking in fear as she walked into the room scowling. She demanded nothing less than perfection and dedication. I was doing all right in her subject, but certainly didn't shine. I was totally flabbergasted when she volunteered to go from high school to high school during her afternoons off to speak, beg and cajole on my behalf after all my applications were rejected on the first round by each of the high schools in which I tried to enrol. It was through her efforts that I was accepted into the Russian high school in an outlying district. Getting into anything was better than nothing, and I was grateful for her efforts.

The most fun we had was with the Russian teachers. Since Russian had become a compulsory subject overnight, the shortage of teachers was acute. To cover the schools, the Ministry of Education transferred the teachers frequently to make it look as if there were an adequate Russian program. In four years, we had no less than twenty Russian teachers and were often without a teacher for weeks. The teachers were an odd bunch. The schools recruited former POWs who spent some months in Siberia, as well as a few Slavic nationals, in spite of their lack of teaching credentials. German and Latin teachers were "retrained" to teach Russian, often being no more than a chapter or two ahead of their pupils. We took advantage of the situation. Each time we got a new teacher, we told him or her we hadn't done more than the first few chapters. So the lessons always began again with chapter one.

Small wonder that after four years of such instruction, we could hardly put together a sentence!

We had one elderly man for a somewhat longer period of time than usual. He tried very hard to teach us, but we soon found out he had no teaching experience, although he seemed to be very knowledgeable in Russian. His efforts to control our bad behaviour and to impart some knowledge, in spite of our lack of interest, were in vain. He was a very heavy man, wide in the rear. We pushed our desks so close together that he couldn't walk between the rows, so we shamelessly cheated on the tests since he couldn't get close enough to notice. I'm sure he knew of our ploy, but I suspect he too was afraid to complain, so he said nothing. He endured our nastiness and ridicule, sometimes losing his patience and yelling red-faced at one of us. One day, when my friend and I talked through the entire hour, the teacher "lost it" and threatened to stuff us into the stove. He was referring to the huge pot-bellied iron monster near the door that the custodian, making his rounds, fed with coal hourly. Those who sat near the stove were cooked, while those near the window froze. From time to time, someone dropped an eraser into the stove, which created such a stench that we had to evacuate the room for airing. The class usually had to be cancelled, and we often saved ourselves from a test by this method.

Another Anni Néni was our colorless language and literature teacher through our last four years. She was plain, unassuming and quiet. I didn't have any strong opinions of her, positive or negative. Her classes were peaceful. She obviously loved her subject because she read the poems with passion, but seldom demanded of us to feel the same. She was there to share her knowledge and it was up to us to partake of it. She poured her wisdom about writing into our silly heads without our notice. Occasionally, we had to write an essay about some subject, such as "How I Spent My Summer Holidays." She read aloud the best works and pointed out what made them stand out from the rest. She never embarrassed a student by reading or ridiculing a poor effort. She only worked with positive reinforcement. One day, she brought back our corrected essays and read the one she thought was the best example of that particular assignment. When she started to read and I realized it was my paper, my color rose with embarrassment and pleasure. To this day, I could rewrite that essay almost verbatim. It was my first success in writing.

Anni Néni managed to infuse me with a love for Hungarian literature, a thirst for a large vocabulary and a clear understanding of what makes a composition interesting. To this day, when I sit down to write, I find her sitting on my shoulder whispering rules of style. I can hear her admonishing me to add color, sound and smell, never use the same word twice, and have balance in my work. When I finish a composition, I ask myself if she would approve. I polish until the answer is yes.

———

Not long ago, I finally picked up the phone in Budapest and told Anni Néni, my Hungarian language teacher, how much I appreciated her for the skills she gave me and how I've been using them for the past four decades. She was pleased even though, as I expected, she didn't remember me at all.

The Redheaded Angel

When people ask me what I remember best about my childhood, and I want to be honest, I must answer, "fear." As a dreamy child, I didn't fit well into the highly structured, strict, almost militaristic Hungarian school system. I hobbled along the best I could. I was always trying to melt into the crowd, lest a teacher take exception to me and reprimand me. I more or less succeeded until Zsuzsi Néni came along as a math and homeroom teacher in grade five. She was an aristocratic beauty who underhandedly defied the equality preached by the regime and favoured the three or four girls of her social class, crumpling the others like so much waste paper into the trash can. She instantly made a pet of the children of "better families," and out of expediency treated the proletariat children well, but scorned the middle class bourgeoisie pupils between. She was supposed to teach us math, but in reality, her mission in life was to rob of self-esteem from those of us with not so lofty breeding. She took a dislike to me on first sight. She was an attractive young woman in her mid twenties, well- dressed and well-groomed, which was odd in those days of government-inspired dowdiness. Life was hell.

She didn't allow me the anonymity of the crowd. At every opportunity, she found fault with me, starting from my appearance and ending with my math skills, bruising my ego at every turn. She regularly picked away at my self-esteem with her red-painted nails. A whiff of her perfume, as she came around the corner, could tie Gordian knots in my stomach. Customarily, the teacher could call upon anyone to give an oral presentation on the previous day's lesson at anytime. We were marked mainly on these oral mini-tests. She called someone up to the board to solve a problem, having them explain aloud each step as they did it. Zsuzsi Néni often interrupted with questions or comments, making them lose their train of thought and thus affecting their performance. She used this weapon to humiliate me to the point where I stood stammering in front of the class like an imbecile, unable to remember my own name, let alone how to solve an equation. At parents' meetings, where children were never present, she was in rare form, unleashing her venomous remarks about me to my mother. Zsuzsi Néni told my mother, in front all the other parents, how stupid and lazy I was in class. When my mother arrived home, she berated me and urged me to change my ways, to try harder so as not to embarrass her the next time. Mother, always ready to yield to any authority, believed Zsuzsi Néni. According to her, all the other parents got glowing reports about their children. I came to hate those evenings and Zsuzsi Néni with a passion, but I was powerless to change either. I wanted to die rather than to face these tongue-lashings. But what could I do? I had no people skills, no sympathetic ear to open my heart to and no one to give me advice.

In grade seven, Zsuzsi Néni managed to convince my mother I needed remedial tutoring in math, insisting I was a slow learner. After two or three sessions with me, the remedial teacher my mother hired informed her that I understood math very well and she didn't feel right about taking her money. Irate, my mother finally stood up to Zsuzsi Néni and demanded that she give me a proper chance, then told me to be prepared for an oral test soon.

The next time I was called to the board, instead of the all-too-familiar lump of fear in my throat, I kept my calm and solved the problem without a flaw, talking continuously, not allowing her a chance to interrupt. She looked at me and announced "A five!" which was equal to an A. "But be sure to tell your mother it was an easy problem!" she added with a sarcastic sneer.

It was with my usual trepidation that I faced grade eight. The high walls of the narrow corridors at school seemed even more formidable than before. The dusty, dingy classroom was full of happily chattering girls as I braced myself for another year of attacks. But instead of Zsuzsi Néni, in walked a very young redhead who introduced herself as Margit Néni, our new math and homeroom teacher. She looked fresh and pretty, as if she'd just stepped out of a Botticelli painting. Next, she opened the dreaded class journal, an old-fashioned ledger-size book where our infractions and marks were recorded for the past three years. She flipped through it for a few seconds and said, "Girls, I'm not going to read your profiles in the journal. From this day on, you are to me who you prove yourself to be." With a grand flourish, she slammed the book shut and blushed.

Right then and there, I realized this lovely, shy teacher would be my salvation and I started to work for her passionately. With her gentle encouragement, one successful oral test followed another. I found that not only did I like math, with its endless opportunities for problem-solving, but I had a strong aptitude for it. I worked in earnest for my self-esteem, as well as to garner that beautiful blushing smile from her.

The next year I moved on to high school. I was turning into a woman. Since money was increasingly short in our home, I had to wear old clothes I had already out grown. They were so tight under my school uniform, a navy smock over regular clothes, that I felt like a sausage about to burst. I had a very nice brown wool dress for going to the theatre, which my aunt had sent from Spain, and the regulation navy blue skirt with a rather tight white blouse for school functions, but spring and summer were approaching and I had nothing else that fit. Heeding my grandmother's oft repeated wisdom, "When you're troubled, go into the first church you pass, pray and contemplate. The answer will come," I looked for a church. The first church in my path was the Franciscan Church in the inner city and I went in. Mid-afternoon during the week, I was the only teenager among five or six old ladies praying in different corners of the church. After a brief amateurish prayer, I sat there half-believing that a solution would come, when suddenly I had the answer. I shot out of the church and headed to Margit Néni's apartment, two or three blocks away. She was quite surprised to see me, but listened patiently while I stammered out my request: "Could you find me a math tutoring position? We're desperately short of money, and I have no clothes to wear in the spring." Although I was still a bit timid about my math because of the emotional beating I had taken from Zsuzsi Néni, I felt I had to be bold and try. Surprisingly, Margit Néni didn't think my request was outrageous and promised to look around.

Within a couple of days, I had a paying student not far from my home. I saved every forint and in the spring, I bought material for a navy blue suit. A distant relative who made her living as a seamstress made the suit for a reasonable price, after I spent hours poring over her fashion magazines to pick just the right style. I felt ravishing in that suit and strutted around with justified pride. The fruit of my first employment!

———

In 1959, still having major problems in English, I entered the all high schools math competition for Manitoba at my teacher's insistence. I came in 76th out of several hundred students, even though I had to skip all the wordy questions because my English wasn't adequate enough to understand them yet. That was my triumph over Zsuzsi Néni.

Sixteen years after finishing grade eight, on my first visit to Hungary, I arranged to see Margit Néni in an elegant café in Budapest. I told her about my math and science success, and that I attributed all my other successes indirectly to her too, because she'd begun the restoration of my self-esteem with her action on that first day of school so long ago. She blushed to the roots of her red hair, and she still looked like a Botticelli angel sent to rescue me when I most needed it.

I carried math right through my University years, earning a bachelor of Science degree with a minor in math, just to prove to myself I was able. In my spare time, I earned good money tutoring math. By my third year, I saved enough to buy my first car, a used Anglia.

We and Us

I often use the expression we or us when I describe some events. That's because I feel I wasn't alone in my experiences. My childhood friends, as far as I know, experienced some of the same feelings. We never talked about them and only made tentative references to them even in later years. Under the communist regime, family problems and day-to-day life were taboo subjects, and that's so ingrained that none of us finds it easy to break that barrier, even after fifty years. Therefore, even though our early lives were very closely entwined, were friends by definition, but not through confidences or mutual support.

From grades one to grade six or seven, Julika and Katalin were my closest friends. We walked home from school together. Julika's father was the custodian of the District Court. Consequently, we had permission to cut through the courthouse on our way to and from school. Sometimes, as a special a treat, supervised by Julika's father, we could ride the Paternoster, a continuous slow-moving elevator, a privilege that few of our peers had! We loved it and bragged about it to our envious classmates.

Every Monday, I had a half-day play date with Julika. We either went to school in the morning or the afternoon. Lack of space in the schools necessitated shifts, which alternated weekly. I rode the elevator to the top floor of the courthouse and knocked on the door marked "Private." The service apartment of the custodian was spacious and sunlit, a sharp contrast to the courthouse with its dim corridors, massive, dark oak doors and intimidating goings on. We instinctively knew not to notice the handcuffed prisoners led to and from the infamous Marko Prison across the street. Of course, we knew there was a prison across the street. The street in that block was chained off to traffic, and heavily armed guards protected the area from intrusion. We had to go the long way around the courthouse to get home if we couldn't cut through the building.

In bad weather, we idled in the solemn vestibule to talk and weave our fantasy tales of being a part of a ballet company. We were three nine year olds, oblivious to the real function of the building and the people in it. None of us ever took ballet or even dance classes, but the story grew each day and details were added until we almost believed it to be true. In good weather, we sat on the elaborate wrought iron fence surrounding the small but well-tended garden of ornamental bushes in front of the courthouse. From there, Katalin and I eventually continued down the street toward our respective homes, passing the Ministry of Mining and Energy, admiring the cars idling in the quiet side street. The chauffeurs leaned against the cars in little groups, smoking and talking. There were very few cars in Budapest in those days, so to see a dozen or so in a row, including a fabulous silver Hudson, built in the late thirties, was a treat.

Sometimes we forgot the time, so engrossed were we in our make-believe tale. One day we stretched the chatting on the garden rail so much that my stepfather Zoli came looking for me. I got a thunderous reprimand on the way home about how worried my family was. That's the only time I remember him being cross with me.

On Mondays in the sanctuary of Julika's home, we played with dolls or sometimes worked on some school project and Julika's mother, a cheerful lady who kept an impeccable home, always had treats for us. They were an easygoing family and I enjoyed being in their home. In later years, Julika's mom took a job as a stenographer at the ÁVO, the equivalent of the Russian KGB, and led us through the elaborate security system to the weekly free movies they showed in their private theatre. While most of these movies were made in the Soviet Union and were shown to evoke feelings of awe and adoration of the superiority of the Soviet system, there was much to be enjoyed and to expand my cultural horizons. My "propaganda filters," by then, were firmly in place and since we couldn't have afforded such a major weekly entertainment, I took the best of the ÁVO offerings to enrich my cultural growth and filtered out the rest. One movie remains in my memory, the life and music of Rimsky Korsakov.

Katalin and her family were very different. I went to play there often, but had to observe very strict rules. Her father was a remote person, an important official at the National Bank, and he was the only person I knew who traveled outside the borders of our country. He brought home a bounty of mechanical pencils, ballpoint pens and candy from Czechoslovakia. They never offered me one of those treats, but Katalin always showed them to me. We had to be extremely quiet when he was home. We could spread out our dolls in a corner of the bedroom, and I had to leave when it was time for lunch. They were devout Catholics, going to the Basilica every Sunday, even when it was unwise to do so, because secret police officers, in civilian clothes, photographed the crowd surreptitiously. Later, this act of defiance cost Katalin dearly.

While these friends were my constant companions, others came and went in my life. My mother encouraged a friendship that never deepened with Magda, whose father was an aircraft engineer. His skills were so essential that the family lived in relative freedom from harassment by the authorities. Magda was just a bit too serious for my liking. On warm days, we played on their patio surrounded by overgrown bushes and weeds. She did really well in school, I suspect because both her mother and father spent a great deal of time discussing schoolwork with her. Whenever I went to play in their home, her sneaky little brother lurked in the shadows of the dingy apartment, listening in on the "girls' conversation," spying. We told him to get out and threatened to tell on him, but a few minutes later we noticed him watching us again from a shadowy corner.

Then there was Marianna. She lived with her mother and her grandmother, not far from us, on the Körút. Rumour had it her father was in America, but no one was sure if he were American-born or a Hungarian who had abandoned his family for the United States. Marianna was probably the best adjusted of us all. She was a marginal student, but a very talented musician. Her family allowed her to play the current hits, which she could reproduce after she had heard them on the radio, while most of us were trying to stay awake, practicing scales and Czerni's piano exercises. I remember one of her birthday parties vividly where we played Post Office, Musical Chairs and Charades amid gales of laughter. I don't remember ever seeing her without a smile or ever hearing her complain.

I wanted to learn to play the piano desperately. Since Mother was an accomplished piano player, I wanted to emulate her and I loved music. Finally, after much begging, Mother agreed to let me take piano lessons from an elderly widow in our apartment building. I enjoyed the lessons, even though the teacher was rather colorless and uninspiring. The problem was that we had no piano. Another neighbour kindly allowed me to practice on hers, but I felt very uncomfortable asking for practice time and played rather awkwardly in front of a stranger. Mother kept promising to buy a piano. She was going to sell a gold cigarette case to do so. The cigarette case was one of the investment pieces my father had bought at an auction before the war. Finally, I agreed to quit my lessons when I realized she'd never part with the cigarette case and she was right: I wasn't making great progress at my piano lessons.

In later years, at about thirteen, when I was allowed to venture alone further from my home, I hung out with Marika, Ági, Zsuzsi, Nicolette and some others who joined our core group from time to time. We met in the afternoons on the promenade by the Danube and walked up and down exchanging gossip, and ogling the boys who were either playing soccer in the park or were clumped in groups on one of the benches ogling us. The Danube, which runs between Pest and Buda, may have been blue in Vienna in Johann Strauss' time, but in my time the slow-moving river always was muddy brown. Ági and Nicholette were much admired by the rest of us because they had boyfriends, whom they met in the short, quiet street behind the former Kuria, the Supreme Court building. The rest of us stood on the corner, acting as lookouts because their parents forbade them to talk to boys and they'd get into major trouble if their parents happened by and spotted them. Most of our talks centered on boys, clothes and sometimes complaints about teachers and marks. However, one sunny afternoon in the fall of 1954, the conversation turned serious. I can't remember who brought it up, but we all agreed we were in deep trouble. We were going to finish grade eight that spring and had to think of our future. Education up to grade eight was compulsory and free, but after that, you had to gain entrance to a high school to continue your education. This law had a ridiculous aspect. Children had to stay in school until they completed grade eight or turned sixteen, whichever came first. As a result, we had a girl in our class who was nearly sixteen, more woman than child, who had failed grade eight several times and only showed up when the principal threatened her mother with persecution for allowing her to be a truant. She had no interest in education, couldn't relate to the much younger children in her class, and sat morose and tight-faced in class. We suspected she worked part-time to help her low-wage mother eke out a marginal living for them.

Since all the girls in our group were part of the distrusted bourgeoisie and some of us had the added black mark of having attended a private or parochial school in grade one, our chances of being accepted in the high school of our choice were slim. The odds improved with superb marks, but marks were by no means a guarantee of acceptance. Two categories of high schools, "real" and "human," existed for general education. The former concentrated on the sciences and math, while the later emphasized languages and social sciences in their coursework. There were some technical schools where you could learn simultaneously a trade, as well as obtain a senior high school matriculation. The technical schools were in high demand, because although the coursework was heavy, the student had no problem finding a job at the end. Since getting into University was even more difficult than to continue after grade eight, a technical school education was a road to a good job. Competition was fierce. First, as in all high schools, they accepted the káder children, no matter what their marks were, and then they assessed those whose parents were party functionaries or had connections to such functionaries.

Often, there was no room left even to consider the group designated as "other." The designation "other" usually meant the members of the bourgeoisie, "intelligentsia" and assorted other "unreliables," such as children of political enemies.

On this sunny afternoon, six of us girls congregated on a park bench. Ignoring the boys this time, we got into a serious conversation and weighed our future and the options to avoid the pitfalls. We agreed that getting into a technical school was almost impossible, although some of us would have liked to become chemical technicians, textile technicians, architectural draftsmen or medical technicians. Our likelihood of enrolling in those schools was very remote. We all wanted at least to get into high school, because without that we faced having to take a job as a shop assistant for starvation wages or work as a construction labourer for a little bit more. While we had our preferences, it mattered little if we got a spot in a "real" or "human" program. Acceptance in one of the high schools depended on the same criteria as those used for technical school, but usually more of the "other" classification gained acceptance. The final decision always rested with the principal of the particular high school.

We had to fill out pages of applications for each school we wished to try to enrol in and attach signatures from teachers, guarantors —preferably some good party official— as well as a complete profile of our activities in school. We weighed our individual and collective chances of obtaining those signatures and decided we could improve our standing a notch in the matter of school activities.

We were, from the early grades on, members of the Young Pioneers, a politicized version of Scouts, because not joining would have been suicidal for us and our families. We attended long political speeches, standing on one foot from exhaustion while the speaker droned on about the "glorious Soviet Union", or how "our pal Rákosi" was building a prosperous future just for us. We also created bulletin boards with pictures and slogans depicting "Father Stalin," the Russian revolution, the splendid cooperative farms, and the heroic factory workers breaking the norm.

We stood in silence, wooden-faced, when the principal announced Stalin's death, repressing our secret feelings of hope, joy or elation at the news. We all did well in not letting our thoughts and emotions get us and our families into trouble. It was difficult, and we all felt a little envious of Teri, a good káder, who broke into huge sobs on hearing the news. We knew she earned some good points for her sobs with the communist members of the school administration.

The week before our conversation about the merits of joining took place, we all received an application form to join the DISZ, the Student Youth Movement, a continuation of the Pioneers for young people who completed grade eight. We could take the form home to fill out. I thought of discussing the matter with my mother, but knew she'd offer little help in making the decision. By that time, the whole business of political astuteness overwhelmed her. She didn't understand what was going on, didn't really want to know and increasingly handed over responsibilities to me. She threw her hands up and left the decision up to me. It was good to get the problem out in the open with my friends and debate the merits of joining. The conclusion was clear. All logic pointed to filling out the application and joining. There were no valid reasons not to, but the possible benefits were definitely worth the effort. We would get some good points in the school activities column of our application forms for high school, which might mean something when it was time for our high school applications to be evaluated. We decided to join the DISZ to show our goodwill to the powers-to-be, in hopes of gaining some advantage for ourselves. It would have been even better to join the KISZ (Communist Youth Movement), but the chance of children of the bourgeoisie gaining acceptance was slim to none.

The next day, each member of our little group handed in her application for DISZ membership and waited for the acceptance letter with baited breath. A few days later each of us received one, which we interpreted optimistically as a sign that our bourgeoisie background was beginning to fade. Little did I know!

The group didn't discuss the matter again. On the appointed day, we met in front of the Kuria for the initiation ceremonies, dressed in the formal attire of the Young Pioneers: navy pleated skirt and white shirt. Ági made a sarcastic remark about "what a dedicated looking group of young communists" we were and we broke into giggles. As with normal teenage girls the world over, the giggles kept on coming and we couldn't stop. The more we tried, the worse we got until Zsuzsi said we must separate for the duration of the ceremony, because we would get into trouble if we couldn't control ourselves during the speeches. We all agreed it would be wise and we should avoid eye contact with all members of our group until after the initiation. The candidates, at least four hundred, were called up individually and were given a pin, a certificate and a handshake. When we filed out of the grand building, we met on the promenade to walk, gossip and look at the boys. We never discussed the ceremony again.

———

Decades later, I found out most of the handcuffed men I passed in the courthouse were political prisoners brought there on drummed-up charges. Their accusers extracted confessions from them with torture, blackmail and threats. They were broken men waiting for their sentence to serve in a prison camp or mine in a remote area, under inhuman conditions that often ended in their death, maiming or at best returning to their families emotionally broken and disturbed forever.

The Kuria I mention in this story is now the Museum of Folk Culture. Incidentally, it was the presidential palace in the movie Evita. It has one of the most impressive interiors in Budapest, with grand sweeping marble stairs, monumental curved columns, and beautiful carved oak woodwork. Whenever I visit the museum, I see each of us standing with serious faces through the long, drawn-out speeches and filing past the dignitaries to receive our little enamelled pin. I have to repress a giggle.

My friend Magda's snoopy little brother became the brilliant inventor of the world famous Rubik's Cube. Magda is a physician. I only know this from other people. I never had the urge to look them up.

Marianna went on to become a piano player, first in nightclubs and later providing afternoon music in elegant coffee shops. Her cheerful disposition made her very popular with the clientele.

Class trip to Visegrád, 1953

"Carefree" Youth

Grades one to eight were the guaranteed right of every citizen, but further education was a privilege. One had to apply to the particular school for admission, and acceptance hinged on one's family background as much as on marks. Reality hit me in the face and I learned to worry when, one after the other, my applications to various schools met with rejection. Two of my teachers, Anni Néni my physics teacher, and Margit Néni I my homeroom teacher, gave up their free afternoons to travel personally to a number of schools to plead my case. Many weeks of dedication on their part finally paid off and I was accepted in a high school in Angyalföld, on the outer edge of the city. The only problem was that it was a bilingual Russian-Hungarian school, and my Russian was deplorable. This school, for me, was only slightly better than nothing. I could only hope that with hard work and luck, I wouldn't fail in the first semester.

In July of 1955, my mother and I and her best friend Mariska, her husband Odon and daughter Jutka rented two rooms in a private home in magical Miskolc-Tapolca for two weeks, where I forgot my problems and restrictions during long walks under the hanging branches of the weeping willows. The smell of petunias permeated the moist air and June bugs lit our paths when Mother and I went for a late evening walk along the creek that ran through the center of the park in the middle of the town. During the day, we swam in one of the three swimming pools.

Miskolc-Tapolca, with its unique swimming pools, is the most beautiful resort in northeast Hungary. There is a warm indoor pool, which goes directly into the mountain cave to the origin of the hot spring. The dim lighting and fluttering bats above make it mysterious and enchanting. For hot days, there's an open-air "strand," several pools surrounded by grass, a paradise for sun lovers and children. A small romantic bath near the caves, with changing rooms built on stilts in the middle of the round pool, was our third choice.

One warm summer evening, a number of acquaintances joined the five of us under the moonlit sky in the garden of the Anna Hotel for refreshments. There was a dance band playing on the bandstand. The music, the weather and the ambiance had promised a pleasurable evening, but I failed to realize until later just how memorable it was. A couple wandered into the garden and while looking for a table, the woman saw Ödön and flew over to envelop him in her arms. It turned out they were old school friends who hadn't seen each other in decades and in the excitement of the reunion, she failed to introduce her husband.

The poor man sat down beside me, and to cover his embarrassment, drew me into a conversation. He asked the usual questions about school and future plans. I, for some unexplainable reason, unburdened all my suppressed fears and trepidations with passion to this sympathetic stranger. When I was finished and spent, he handed me a business card and told me to have my mother visit him just as soon as we returned to Budapest. In the dark of the garden, I couldn't make out the words, so it wasn't until much later that Mother and I read the card in our room. I had just unloaded all my problems and fears to the Chief Ombudsman of the City of Budapest! Naturally, Mother rushed to see him as soon as we arrived back.

The next day, I was enrolled in the Kossuth Zsuzsanna Girls' Real Gymnasium —High School— near my home. This school was my first choice, but the principal had rejected my application. I was elated, though I knew things weren't going to be easy. The principal of the school, a Mrs. Otta, wife of a high-ranking political officer in the army, was an infamous communist and wasn't thrilled to have me enter by the back door when she'd already thrown me out the front door. I was sure she'd make my life as miserable as possible, but if I were careful to spew the right communist propaganda at the right time, never get into a discussion and work hard at my studies, I'd survive and might even get my senior matriculation.

Mrs. Otta, determined to find a way to have me out of there before I could graduate, made my life hell. Prowling the halls in her distinctive grey satin robe, Mrs. Otta sent shivers up our backs wherever she went. Her piercing eyes could pick out a student from the crowd for a minor infraction and have her report to her office before anyone knew what happened. A couple of those and you were out. I'm sure the teachers feared her just as much as the students did. There was a palpable atmosphere of distrust, fear and suspicion hanging like a thick curtain, isolating each person from the other. In Ideology —current affairs— class, Mrs. Otta entered the class noiselessly after everyone was in their places, sat in the back row and observed. Then at the end of the class she made cutting remarks about anyone who hadn't actively participated in the discussion or who veered away from the official party line. I was petrified. I was certain she was there to single me out and find the flaw that would make it possible for her to get rid of me.

The halls were very quiet during recess. There were no gaily chatting groups, no peer interaction, no talking to teachers — not even about schoolwork. Everyone was determined to mind his own business and keep her nose clean. I didn't know anyone in the school, so I had no idea which classmate could be trusted. By watching and listening to the meagre conversation, I determined who was a good káder and cultivated those friendships to show the principal I wasn't as bad as my political pigeonhole made me. I hoped to improve my bourgeois image by socializing with the "right people." I consciously set my preferences aside to better my political position, a sad necessity for a fourteen year old. I was very lonely.

We wore a navy blue lab-coat-like blue smock with a white collar and a navy tam with the school crest pinned to the front. If the principal noticed your white collar wasn't clean or a bit crumpled, she sent you to the office. Bangs she considered "a capitalist holdover," so any hair falling over the forehead must be pinned back. The tam had to be centered on the forehead. Anyone caught wearing the tam at a rakish or more fashionable angle, even several miles from school, was called into the principal's office. Assembly in the draughty marble entrance hall was a very serious and formal affair that took place right after the first bell every Monday morning. Since the principal gave her speech right in front of the only door leading into the school, heaven help the student who was late. Since no one ever dared to talk about their punishment, I could only surmise from the tearstained faces of classmates that it was severe. I lived within easy walking distance, but many of the girls hailed from districts far away, travelling by several changes of streetcar for as much as an hour and a half to get school. Any number of hold-ups could occur in peak traffic.

We had some outstanding teachers, although they were cold and impersonal. I joined the Art History Club, an extracurricular study group directed by one of our teachers. She had us research our chosen topics, give reports, and patiently worked with each of us so we could develop our special interest to whatever degree we wished. I loved those study afternoons and got quite interested in the variety of architectural styles that were represented in the streetscape of Budapest. I was particularly interested in the Roman, gothic and renaissance architecture, the remains of which were readily visible in the Buda Castle District. I had to beg my mother to go see the ruins. She couldn't understand my attraction to "those piles of stones."

The music teacher organized an occasional dance afternoon when boys from another high school were invited. The dances were held in the unadorned, dusty music room to the tune of some scratchy old records. The tense, fearful mood of the girls of Kossuth Zsuzsanna did nothing to encourage the awkward boys to dance. All of these socials were a flop, as far as I can remember.

Each school had a doctor and nurse assigned to hold office hours once a week. These professionals administered the compulsory vaccinations, gave cursory check ups, checked students who had just came back from a lengthy illness and gave lectures on health. They also scheduled visits for the entire school to have their annual chest X-ray. Tuberculosis was endemic and the government was determined eradicate the disease with continuous testing.

The doctor and nurse in my elementary school were very pleasant and I had the good fortune to have the same team assigned to my high school. With all the coolness, fear and suspicion, it was nice to see two trustworthy, friendly faces. I didn't hesitate to sign up when they announced this duo was offering a Red Cross first aid course for anyone who wished to be trained. I hoped such a volunteer activity would impress Mrs. Otta and earn me credits with her.

The material was horribly outdated. For instance, we had to learn how to deal with mustard gas victims, but the two warm and pleasant ladies made it enjoyable. Since I was the only one from my class who completed the course, I automatically became the first aid officer for that class. The idea was that the first aid officer would look after any student who was injured in the classroom. Most of the injuries were cuts from razor blades we used for sharpening pencils, because few students had pencil sharpeners. Sprains in physical education, upset stomachs, and slivers from desks or the floor were the other common problems. Since we had no kits available, treating a cut meant tearing a strip from someone's clothing to create a bandage. The Central Ambulance Service of Budapest was across the street from the school and had an outpatient clinic. I usually applied pressure with my hand, and walked the injured classmate across the street for proper treatment and waited until I could walk her back.

The waiting room of the ambulance service was entertainment in itself. Since we were next to the District Court and jail, often families who attended a trial left the courtroom after the verdict and physically settled their differences on the street. Battered and bleeding "warriors" waited for treatment, still yelling and swearing at the other group, who were also waiting for treatment. The ambulance people just shrugged. Their job was to patch them, not to mete out justice.

Thus in constant fear, with a bit of shrewdness and a huge dose of prudence, I survived my first year of high school.

Young Adult

Cultural Events

While there was a shortage of material goods, there were a number of cultural benefits available freely or cheaply, especially for children. Either as a class outing or with a group of friends during school holidays, we visited the many world-class museums and exhibits in and around Budapest. Frequently, we had the opportunity to see special exhibits created by one of the museums or those visiting from another socialist country.

One of the displays I remember was about the achievements of Michurin. Michurin, an uneducated Soviet horticulturist, became a hero and received the order of Lenin and the Order of the Red Banner of Labour for his achievements in plant genetics. He believed, contrary to Mendel's experiments, that acquired characteristics can be inherited. Michurin's theories, elaborated by Trofim D. Lysenko, were adopted by the Soviet government as fact and put into practice. It was a uniquely communist approach to agriculture. They claimed Michurin-style research yielded super crops that made the inhospitable Siberian plain a virtual paradise for agriculture. I enjoyed the photos of the Siberian landscape and the description of the lives of its inhabitants. Even at age ten, without much understanding of plant husbandry and genetics, I knew better than to believe Michurin would create a paradise overnight.

Even a fool could see government promises and reality were two different things. The newspapers talked about how improving infrastructure in rural areas—newly built roads, running water, and sewers—would make the lives of villagers easier. Reality was different. When Mother, Mariska, Jutka and I rented a room in a farmhouse near Lake Balaton, the streets were rutted dirt that turned to slippery mud after a rain, and the outhouse was fly-infested and smelly. We were lucky if an old newspaper was available for use as toilet paper. We were experts in crumpling newsprint until it became soft enough to use on our intimate parts. Paper was so scarce, it was used as many times as possible for different functions.

On one summer vacation, I was supposed to look after the much younger Jutka while both our mothers had an afternoon nap. She went to the outhouse, came flying out and headed directly to the lake, some ten minutes' walk away. I ran after her, worried about being scolded, for we were supposed to stay in the farmyard and not go to the lake on our own. Jutka rushed into the lake and no amount of talk would bring her out. I stood there cajoling, begging, and threatening, to no avail. Eventually, I pried the woeful tale out of her. She went to the outhouse and used some newsprint that was previously used as a drop cloth while cleaning hot peppers. The poor child was in agony.

Most of my knowledge of what was true and what was propaganda came from a weekly humour and political cartoon magazine, the Ludas Matyi. I was a devotee of the magazine. The paper hit the newsstands at one o'clock Wednesday afternoons and was sold out by two o'clock. Nothing could keep me from being at the newsstand on time. At first, the coloured drawings in this distinctly colorless society, attracted me. Later, I realized they were a way to the truth through humour.

Apparently, Stalin, who wasn't afraid of sending thousands of academics, political rivals and writers to the gulag or to the gallows, was afraid of the humorists' pen. He thought they'd be kinder to him if he allowed them relative freedom. Thus, the Krokodile in the Soviet Union was allowed to flourish as long as it balanced criticism of the state with ardent hatred of the so-called "Imperialist West." The Ludas Matyi was the same. Ironically, I learned about life in the USA, the Korean War and President Eisenhower from these cartoons and from the humorous essays. Starving men and women cowered in the shadow of skyscrapers, while cigar chomping, fat industrialists drove by them in great finned cars. The message was, "Eisenhower and Churchill plotted to colonize the world, while Tito, their vicious chained dog, frothing at the mouth, did their bidding." In contrast, every time Hungary, Hungarians or their Eastern Block allies achieved a goal, no matter how small or how big, the papers reported it as another slap in the face for Eisenhower. This was great fodder for the funny paper. I learned to read between the lines, separate the propaganda from the facts, and got a fairly good handle on international events and politics.

Inexpensive tickets to all kinds of cultural events were made available for children. I saw more live theatre as a child than many North American adults do in a lifetime. One of the most memorable plays I attended was Sophocles' "Antigone." Several classmates and I sat mesmerized on the third balcony, from where the actors were like ants on the stage, during this powerful production by the top dramatic actors and actresses in the National Theatre.

I also had a season ticket for a Saturday afternoon music series in the Liszt Ferenc Academy. They designed a program especially to teach the history of classical music styles to ten to fifteen year olds. It was an interactive programme where the young audience joined the musicians in singing some parts of the performance. The musicians were the leading artists in their specialty. The most impressive occasion was when we learned about Beethoven. The audience of three hundred children, accompanied by the state philharmonic orchestra, sang with gusto the words to Schiller's "Ode to Joy" from Beethoven's Ninth Symphony.

My much-admired cousin Tomi was studying to become a conductor at the Liszt Ferenc Academy of music. In spite of the rift in the family, caused by my mother's decade-old disagreement with Uncle Gyula, Tomi always made sure each of the cousins had a free ticket to his concerts. Two of my aunts and Uncle Gyula still refused to recognize me, but I truly enjoyed watching my talented cousin's performances.

Workers in factories, collective farms, and large companies could often buy cheap tickets to cultural events from the social organizer of the firm. It wasn't unusual to see a large bus drive up to the steps of the Opera and disgorge a group of farmers for the evening. My stepfather, trying his mightiest to be a responsible adoptive father after the divorce, managed to get coveted tickets to see the Moisejev Ballet's dazzling performance held in an open-air stadium. Wrapped in warm clothes, I watched breathlessly the stunning folk dance production on the distant stage. Zoli also managed to get a hold of an occasional ticket for operettas. I loved the shows at the Operetta Theatre. The stories were fanciful, the costumes rich and decadent, the music melodious and the theatre full of gilt, velvet and plush, a remnant of the past where counts and countesses cavorted without restraint.

At least once a year, we were able to ride the narrow-gauge Young Pioneer train built in the Buda Hills. The train meandered through the lovely hills, stopping at several stations where we could buy refreshments and eat our packed sandwiches. Children ten to fourteen years old operated the train. We watched as smartly uniformed kids seriously gave orders over the telephones in the glass-enclosed control room of the station, throwing big, important switches and tapping out messages in Morse code. We could even send a postcard or a telegram from the station's post office where young postmasters and postmistresses worked earnestly.

We often went for school outings. For hands-on experience in botany, we went to Hüvösvölgy, a suburb, by streetcar and walked across the weedy meadow to Hármashatár Mountain. We searched for various plants, dug them out, and dried them for our plant collection folios. We noted the root system, leaves and flowers. Unfortunately, the trail was so packed from continuous traffic and the knives we carried from home so primitive, we seldom succeeded in digging out anything without damaging the specimen. Concrete wartime bunkers dotted the trail that our teachers feared might still have live ammunition or bombs, so they were out of bounds. We longed to explore them and play hide-and-seek in these labyrinths, but those who tried faced severe punishment. Going down the mountain, in the cool shade of the trees with only a shaft of sunshine breaking through the thick canopy of leaves and the crunching sound of twigs and dead leaves underfoot, was always my favourite time of the day.

My husband was one of the Young Pioneer Train staff. His memories of those days are the highlight of his childhood. On every trip to Hungary, we must hop on the train, still run by children, for a sentimental journey. He insists on talking to the ten-year-olds working there and telling them he was one of the young controllers when the train opened in 1948. They stare at him, speechless. It seems like ancient history to them.

My love of live theatre remains. Budapest still has a dozen or more stages playing nightly, and we take in as many productions as possible on every trip.

Eva on Castle Hill overlooking the Danube

The Other Penguin

No story of my early life could be complete without mentioning Nene, my honorary grandmother. I felt unconditional love of this serene woman. Nene was my grandmother's first cousin, a childless war widow with infinite love and patience for children.

Before me, she "adopted" her sister Szera's granddaughter, Zsuzsa, as her own grandchild, giving her the limitless attention, love and homespun wisdom of her heart. As Zsuzsa, ten years my senior, grew up and became busy with boys and parties, Nene turned her attention to me. She took me to visit distant relatives and explained how they fitted into the family. She sparked my interest in genealogy.

Nene's own place became uninhabitable during the battle of Budapest, so for a few months, she lived with us, and then moved in with her sister Szera. Nene's gentle ways helped reduce the tension between my mother, my grandmother and my grandfather. Defending each without hurting the other wasn't easy. Both Mother and Grandmother tried to be in charge, and my grandfather was very difficult to handle because of his advanced Alzheimer's disease. Whenever Nene sensed the start of a disagreement, she'd either head to the basement to fetch some firewood to stay out of the storm —a tough task for a woman over sixty, hauling it up to the third floor— or went to the kitchen to create something for my grandmother, hoping to appease her that way. Grandmother loved food, but things had to be made just so or she wouldn't eat them. Ingredients in those days were scarce and Grandmother was hard to please, especially in a pique, so Nene was rarely successful at using this technique to diffuse the situation. Mother was easier to calm. If Nene could turn the conversation to fashion or reminiscences of the old days when Mother prepared for a ball in an elegant dress, Nene could sidetrack her from the fight.

She was kind and gentle to my grandfather, who became more and more confused every day. She patiently taught me how to lace up his boots, a task I loved to perform for him every morning. Nene was my grandmother's assistant in her store for forty years. She was used to her demands, unreasonable at times, and never complained. She was a great listener. I don't remember her ever openly giving me advice; she just listened intently and made suggestions.

In contrast to serene Nene, her two sisters remain a comic relief in my memory. Szera was vivacious and full of good humour. She coined the family phrase, "I have so much to do, I think I'll have a nap." According to family lore, she uttered this on the afternoon before her wedding. I remember on one visit to her home, she served a platter of brownie-like squares with white specks on top. Laughingly, she explained she forgot to add the baking powder and decided to sprinkle it on top. They were terrible, but she was unflappable. We simply refused seconds.

The other sister Paula, affectionately called Palika, was the eldest. She must have been well into her eighties when I was in my early teens. Her home was at the other end of Budapest, over an hour on foot. We lived halfway between her and her son's place. Every week, she spent Sunday lunch with her son, Tibor, and daughter-in-law, Ilus. Each time she left, he gave her money to take the tram the following week. Every Sunday morning, like clockwork, she arrived at our place, her face made up with quantities of rouge embedded in her wrinkles, eyes bright, a little out of breath, and she plunked herself down on the sofa, dressed in a threadbare brown dress that begged for the attention of a dry cleaner. Then she hauled her huge, battered crocodile purse unto her lap, from which after several minutes of feverish digging she produced a chocolate bar for me. There was another chocolate bar in the cavernous purse for her "little boy," Tibor. Every week she used her streetcar money to buy the sweets. No amount of begging her to spare herself the two-hour walk deterred her from repeating the feat the following Sunday. She was an independent spirit, no one could tell her how to live her life, and she lived it to the fullest.

In comparison to the sisters, Nene was calm and conservative. She wore no makeup and usually dressed in black with a white jabot at her throat, like my grandmother. That's why my mother teasingly coined the nickname for them, "the two penguins."

When I picked up the navy suit from the seamstress, bought with my earnings from my tutoring job, I was walking on air. I thought it was the most wonderful garment in the world. As I headed home with my precious suit, I passed the Western Railroad Station and almost automatically walked into the notions store next to it. The store was old and dingy, catering mainly to farmers who shopped there before taking the train back to their village. Nene worked there. When Grandmother lost her store to nationalization, Nene got a job as clerk in this shop, close to where we lived. All the other clerks knew me, since I often stopped by for a quick visit of my "extra-grandmother."

On that day, they directed me to the basement of the store where Nene stood in the middle of the floor, her head covered with a bandana, stuffing feathers into a pillowcase. As always, her face lit up with the broad smile reserved just for me. She examined the suit carefully and pronounced it beautiful. She was also impressed that I had earned the money for it myself. "You need a pale blue silk blouse to go with this," she commented.

"I spent all my money on the material and the seamstress, Nene. It will have to wait. In the meantime, because it's unlined, I can wear the suit as a two piece dress," I replied. A mysterious smile crossed her face as I kissed her and bid her goodbye.

Two weeks later, Nene arrived unexpectedly, carrying a small parcel wrapped in tissue paper. It was a pale blue sleeveless silk blouse with tiny white swirls printed on it. I was speechless. I knew she didn't have a spare penny, let alone money for the blouse. She said she made it from some remnants she found. On closer examination, it was obvious she told the truth. While she cut the front in the regular manner, the back was made of six or seven narrow strips, carefully sewn together like a quilt. To me, it was beautiful and very special, because I knew every stitch had with it her boundless love.

———

The notions store stood where today's large western-style West End Mall stands, proclaiming the success of the market driven economy.
Nene is long gone, but I keep in close touch with her other favourite, Zsuzsa. As she describes it, "You need a pair of binoculars to find the kinship between us," but our attachment and love for this very special woman binds us tighter than genes could.
Due mainly to Nene's influence, I've recently taken up genealogy as hobby.

Irene, Eva, Jutka and Mariska, summer 1955

Shrinking Circumstances

It seemed to me parts of the furnace were always out in the yard every winter, waiting for repair. At first, we heated the kitchen with the gas oven, making a beeline for the frozen bed when it was time to go to sleep. Later, many of the tenants acquired potbelly stoves, which they vented into inadequate chimneys or into the airing shafts that ran between apartments connecting the bathrooms. It's a miracle we survived such dangerous practices without carbon monoxide poisoning or a fire. There was no hot water at all. The useable parts of the central hot water heater went to try to keep the furnace alive, without much success. Although we had a fully equipped bathroom, in winter we washed in a basin of water heated on the stove in the relatively warm kitchen.

Once or twice a winter, we went to the Gellért Baths and rented a sunken bathtub. Mother and I would loll in the hot water for an hour, then the attendant would wrap us in hot, crisp, starched sheets and we had a nap in the resting room.

After the war, destruction from bombings and the streaming masses of country folk moving to Budapest in search of employment caused a severe accommodations shortage and a housing crisis. At first, the government requisitioned "surplus" rooms in private homes. Surplus meant any room over what was needed by the family. The housing authority assessed the need as one room for parents, one for all the children, or one room for three or four relatives of the same sex. The windowless half-room that many of the apartments, including ours, had as a connecting hall didn't count as a room The requisitioned room became the property of the co-tenants, often a couple. They shared kitchen and bathroom facilities, and often the co-tenant, because of the layout of the apartment, had to walk through part of the original owners' rooms to get to their own. These forced communal homes were disastrous. The constant clashes of authority, lack of privacy and use of shared space created a war zone in many homes. A whole book could be written about the horrible fights between people forced to share this way.

For a while, Mother avoided the problem by swapping the maid's room for cleaning, but when she divorced my stepfather, it became obvious it was only a matter of time before we'd be forced into a co-tenancy. Three women —Grandmother, Mother and I— according to the law should share one room. Our apartment was two and a half rooms, plus a maid's room. Mother decided to voluntarily offer up a room and the bathroom, and with a similar offer from our next door neighbour, who was also afraid of a forced roommate, a third little apartment was created. We'd have a new bathroom built in the former maid's room. The windowless half-room would serve as mother's stocking repair shop cum living room, and the three of us would share the one bedroom.

We lived in construction debris for what seemed to be months. In the end, the maid's room off the kitchen became our new bathroom and Mother, Grandmother and I shared the one bedroom. We had dust everywhere and had to do without a bathtub for a long time. Even after the tub was installed in our new bathroom, we had to clean it nightly because of the dirt, debris and dust left behind by the construction crews still working, finishing walls, flooring and installing the sink. Cleaning the tub became my job. I hated to do this nightly ritual of sweeping out plaster and dust, then scrubbing with a kind of fine sand sold house to house by men from the Swabisch villages near the capital. The improvement was that we installed a small manifold water heater and no longer had to carry pots of boiling water from the kitchen to take a bath in three inches of water.

Later, in 1954, the water of the natural hot spring from Margit Island was piped into the apartment buildings that were near the Danube in Pest. This was truly a blessing. I had suffered from joint pain and inflammation for years, and just about at the same time a specialist prescribed a series of hot baths in spa water as a medication. Going to the baths two or three times a week would have been time- consuming and far too expensive. The hot water from the island had the same composition as the spa waters, complete with the sickening smell of sulphur, and it flowed from the tap three times a week. Although it didn't cure my joints, the hot water certainly helped ease the pain.

Cleaning the bathtub reminds me of the scouring powder sellers who entered an apartment building and hollered, "Reibsand, köpor!" in singsong fashion from the middle of the courtyard. They sold a natural scouring powder, the precursor to Comet or Old Dutch, mined in the neighbouring Buda Hills. Several vendors visited the apartment buildings regularly. The men selling potatoes announced their presence in similar fashion, and so did the junk buyer, the rag rug maker and the pot repairer. That last one really fascinated me. He set up camp in the courtyard and people with leaky pots came and had the hole repaired. He cut two patches, one for inside the vessel and one for the outside, carefully joined them with a small spike and a drop or two of solder, then banged away at the patch with his hammer until he made a watertight seal of the malleable metal patches.

The building was always noisy. The postman announced his presence at the top of his lungs daily and the occasional organ grinder set up in the courtyard to play his dilapidated instrument for donations. At the end of his performance, he removed his greasy hat and took a comical, deep bow, while his eyes were turned upward to see how many had turned out to appreciate his art. He was usually rewarded with a few paper-wrapped coins the audience tossed from above.

Then there was the iceman. We used iceboxes, the kind you see in museums nowadays. In the summer, he came daily with a horse-drawn cart loaded with blocks of ice. His shouts mobilized the neighbourhood, as young and old hurried with buckets to get a chunk from the dripping wagon. The pail was heavy and usually banged against my leg as I struggled carrying it home. The icebox residing in our pantry had a little spigot on the bottom to drain off spent ice water that collected in a tray and I had to carry it to the kitchen sink to empty, preferably without spilling. I seldom managed this feat without at least a few drops on the black and white checkerboard stones of the kitchen floor, which then had to be wiped up with a floor rag wrapped around an old broom.

When the construction was finished, we had a nice, comfortable apartment and as Mother used to say, "I'd rather live in a cubicle by myself, than to share a palace with someone else." A seemingly nice young couple moved into the new apartment. Nobody trusted them. Only people with party connections had a chance to apply and receive such accommodations. The new apartment was now the property of the city, to give to whomever they thought suitable. Therefore, the young couple must have been highly connected, and might even be informers. I thought they seemed to be shy more than anything. She was, we were told, very ill with asthma and we seldom saw her, but I often saw him shaking out the dusting rag or carrying groceries home. We exchanged pleasant "hellos," but never stopped to talk.

In our own apartment, we rearranged the furnishings to fit our shrunken circumstances. The wide windowsill that covered the radiators became my desk for doing homework. When I opened the latticed doors in front, my chair fitted nicely under the sill and there was even a ledge to rest my feet. I usually drew back the long lace curtains to get more of an open feeling and to spread my books and tools. I loved this spot. It was bright, and I could see the goings- on in the street below. It was a quiet street and I knew nearly all the people who traveled back and forth on it. I had the radio tuned to the latest popular songs, head bent over my books. Like any teen, I loved to listen to music while I did my home homework.

The few people who entered the low warehouse across the street and left soon after created most of the traffic. It was the home of Szidike and Mrs. Nagy, who took in washing. The two women were sisters, but for some reason, Szidike, the public relations person of the small enterprise, always referred to her silent sister as Mrs. Nagy, yet never used her own last name. They lived on the far side of the sunny paved courtyard. An oleander tree bloomed in a bucket in front of the door, a pleasant surprise in this concrete jungle. However, all pleasantness ended there. The small, dim kitchen with its smell of lye and coarse soap, enveloped in a perpetual fog of steam, wiped out all illusions. A smiling Szidike was bent over the ironing board, slinging the heavy iron filled with charcoal embers over crisply starched sheets. She greeted visitors, while the shadow of Mrs. Nagy in the background stirred pots of laundry or bent over the scrubbing vat. I took our bedding and other large items there, since we had no laundry facilities. The old laundry room in the basement of the apartment building still had its coin-operated cauldron for boiling clothes, but the drying room was dusty from disuse. Gone were the maids to do this heavy manual labour. The government-run laundry down the street shredded the clothes, so the little entrepreneurs across the street did a brisk business.

As a result of losing a room, the crystal chandelier that had once graced the sitting room hung right over our beds after the reconstruction. One morning in early summer of 1956, I awoke to the peal of bells. As I rubbed sleep out of my eyes, trying to understand the unusual noise, I looked up to see the chandelier swinging wildly over my head, the shiny drops of crystal banging against each other. Just then, I realized my immovably solid walnut bed was rocking, too. Mother was already up and turning on the radio to find out what was happening. Almost immediately, we heard the report that there was an earthquake in Budapest, with its epicentre in the southern district of Soroksár. Major damage was restricted to that suburb, but people all over the city felt the shock. That incident, plus the many hours I spent atop a ladder washing the crystal baubles one by one with alcohol during spring cleaning, has put me off crystal chandeliers for life.

Summer Job

My mother and her cousins held get-togethers monthly, each time in someone else's apartment, which were great fun for me. I was included in the gatherings, because at fourteen, they considered me almost grown up. I looked forward to the next gathering. I loved all of the cousins. I had a special relationship with Luli, of whom I'll talk about in a later chapter in detail.

There was Tibor and his wife Ilus, who were very close to my mother. They were childless and treated me as if I were theirs. Tibor got down on the floor to build castles from blocks or to show me how to use my toy accordion. He was my father figure. I spent most of my early years on Tibor's lap. When I grew older, Tibor taught me about photography and talked about his travels when he was young. Ilus was my mother's close friend and confidante. I often went to their home and helped Ilus with some of her chores. She was the first to notice sewing wasn't my forte. She teased me mercilessly about how awkwardly I held the needle when trying to sew on a button. This was all done in fun without wounding, and we laughed until our sides hurt.

Pista was the black sheep of the family. He was an exceptionally handsome man with a permanent mischievous twinkle in his eye. If there was a lull in the conversation, we could count on him to make a witty remark or do something outrageous like stirring his coffee with his pinkie. Apparently, he was a wild one, a rogue, in his youth. No one gave me details of his exploits, and now in his forties, no one knew just how much to trust him. He was a political officer in the Hungarian army, a typical opportunistic supporter of the regime. There were whispers behind his back, but I never found out what his position meant. His wife, a high-ranking police officer, generally sat in a corner with a serious face, watching and listening, but seldom participating in the conversation. I understood that at these gatherings talking politics was taboo, for no one was sure about those two.

Wearing my new suit with the blue silk blouse and my newfound confidence, I went to the gathering where I was duly admired. Pista asked me what I was going to do during the summer holidays, and I told him I'd love to get a job to earn some more money for more clothes, but I had no connections. He said he'd take care of that if I'd like to work in a greenhouse. I agreed immediately and I eagerly anticipated becoming a working woman. Then, suddenly, my hopes collapsed. Pista got sick and was in the military hospital. There were a lot of whispers among the adults about Pista's "condition." The next Sunday, we went to the hospital to visit him. In the foyer, we were instructed to strip off all our clothes and were given gowns to wear to the ward. We thought he must be seriously ill. It turned out he was in fine shape on the mental ward. There seemed to be nothing wrong with him. Someone in the family thought he might have found himself in a sticky situation and pretended to have a mental breakdown to avoid the problem.

When he was released from the hospital, he sent me a note with the name and address of the greenhouse and instructions on when to go and see his friend. I was very excited the morning I took the streetcar to Zugliget. I felt as if all eyes were on me, admiring me for being such a grown-up woman of fourteen and a half to take on a real job.

When I arrived at the greenhouse, the place was in turmoil. Several people were shouting, a few girls I judged to be eighteen or nineteen were crying, and the boys looked thunderous. A muscular boy of about eighteen asked me what I was doing there. I told him I was looking for a job. He held me by the shoulder and led me outside. "These people are slave drivers. We're all being fired because we couldn't keep up with their demands. You wouldn't last a day. Take my advice and find another job." Looking at the red-faced foreman, shouting and waving his fist, I decided to take his advice and with deflated spirit, I trudged home.

Our neighbour, who lived in the new apartment created from our extra room, was shaking a dusting rag in front of his suite. I only knew him to say hello and had never talked to him before. He asked me how I was and I, straightforward as usual, told him I was very depressed about the events of the morning, because I was really hoping to make some money. He told me to be at his office in the Ministry of Agriculture first thing in the morning and, "We'll see what we can do." Since he didn't tell me much about his plans, I didn't go with great expectations, but I thought it was very nice of a near- stranger to even offer to try to make me feel better.

The next day I went to the Ministry, asked to see him and was ushered into his office. Even without much experience in these matters, I could see he had to be important to rate such a spacious, well-furnished office. He made a phone call to someone and after much friendly cajoling, he got the person on the other end to see me and hire me if she liked me. I was to go to the College of Horticulture and ask for Mrs. Horvath, right away. I kept my hopes in check as I traveled across the city and climbed the steep street to the College —surrounded by fruit farms, not very far from one of the main squares of Buda. The building itself was encouraging. It was a pleasant, modern building of pleasing architecture nestled into the side of the hill with beautiful vistas from its south-facing windows. Mrs. Horvath was a friendly woman of about twenty-five and very pregnant. She told me she wasn't going to take on one more summer student, but my neighbour, in charge of educational institutions at the Ministry, convinced her to give me a try.

I was to start the next morning, but before that, I had to obtain a letter from my school that certified I had no prescribed summer school studies and that they allowed me to take a job. This was the law. It was with some trepidation I went to the school office to request authorization. There were several students with the same request ahead of me, and I heard the principal severely questioning them and turning some of them down for the permission. By this time, my legs were like rubber bands and

130

butterflies were having a jamboree in my stomach. Here I had managed to stay out of the way of the feared principal all year, only to have to face her to ask for her permission to work. The friendly secretary gave me an encouraging wink when it was my turn to go before the principal. Mrs. Otta turned her steely eye on me, asked a few questions, and told me to make sure I did a good job that wouldn't embarrass the school. With that, she handed me the signed form letter and I was on my way. I could hardly sleep that night from excitement.

I got up early, wore my only skirt, a freshly pressed printed cotton one, with a crisp white blouse. The air smelled clean and fresh when I boarded the streetcar. As the tram chugged along the familiar streets, I was full of expectations. Even the Danube, normally brown, looked blue to me that morning. I arrived at the end of the line too early, so I looked around on the busy square and discovered a stand-up restaurant where one could buy a latte made from recycled, once-used espresso coffee grounds for one forint, an amount even I could afford. I bought one and enjoyed the rare treat. Coffee was so precious that when adults could get it, they didn't waste it on children. We drank a coffee-like concoction of Postum with chicory, which was supposed to taste just like coffee, but didn't. Now I really felt grown up as I walked up the hill to report for work. Another student, Judit, was starting in the same laboratory, so the administrator processed us together. When we handed in our permission letters, hers had an added request by the school for a report on her work at the end of the summer. Mrs. Horvath asked if she could send one to my school, too. Half-listening while taking in all the new impressions, I nodded.

Judit and I were set to work washing test tubes. There were several laundry baskets full, so we didn't run out of work for many days. We laughed and joked while working and always had an encouraging word from someone passing through. It didn't bother me that Judit didn't work as hard as I did. Her father was a big director in the government, and that's how she had obtained the job. She didn't have to exert herself. I was just a little mouse who had lucked out and I was going to show my appreciation. Soon, we were separated. Judit's work was in one room, and I got to work right under Mrs. Horvath's nose in her laboratory cum office. She taught me to use the microtome to cut sections of grape embryos embedded in wax. She praised my work and I enjoyed the challenge of moving the knife smoothly to get long strips of sections sliding off the steel. Then, I was taught to stain and cover the slides I made. She praised me and often dragged in her colleagues to show them the quality of my work. I really didn't know what all the fuss was about, I just knew I liked the challenge, tried to follow directions, do as good a job as I could, and people were nice to me.

For lunch, Judit, Vali, the young secretary and I went down to the Agricultural College where we bought a substantial meal, albeit not very well prepared, for a few forints. Coming back up the hill, we sang the popular songs of the era. After lunch, quite often, we had to eat pounds of peaches or apricots the gardener brought up from one of the orchards, so the pits could be used for experiments. What hardship!

Once or twice, I accompanied Mrs. Horvath to a distant orchard to pick fruit and make notes on the progress of some of the experimental trees. On these outings, in our perfect privacy, we talked about personal things. I found out she too had been brought up by her widowed mother under difficult circumstances, resulting in a similarity of our outlook on life. She was getting less and less mobile as the summer wore on and I often ran errands for her, like buying movie tickets, during my lunch break. Her appreciation for these little tasks showed up as "overtime" on my pay slips.

We needed egg albumin for the slides, but getting an egg was a major undertaking in those days. She sent me to the market to stand in line to buy an egg for the laboratory, but told me not to bother to come back, to simply bring the egg the next day. I noticed these requests always fell on very hot days, so I could go to the swimming pool for the rest of the afternoon. I was sad to see the summer end. I never before felt so secure and liked.

A few days later, I was back to school and in uniform lining up for the opening ceremonies in the dingy, walled-in courtyard. I prepared to daydream through the entire boring affair, when I heard my name mentioned and my ears perked up. The severe principal had a smile on her face, and read the glowing letter from Mrs. Horvath about my work performance to the entire school. She said all students should strive to make the school and her so proud. My life changed at that moment. I think even a little sunshine glinted into the courtyard, reflected from a classroom window above. I no longer had to slink around avoiding the principal and maybe, just maybe, she would let me get my senior matriculation in her school

Graduation ceremony after grade eight

Money, Connections, Privilege

After the communist takeover of the government, with nationalization and the policy of calling the members of the former middle class bourgeoisie, everyone in my circle became poor.

Dressing fashionably was also considered a remnant of bourgeois values or, worse yet, the influence of the imperialist west. Conforming dowdiness became the norm. Nearly everyone, men and women, wore the ubiquitous green coat made of a tough weatherproof woollen fabric, loden. Men wore a navy tam and women had kerchiefs. Fashion- conscious women set themselves apart with unique hand-painted kerchiefs or a colourful custom-knitted pair of wool gloves. There was hardly anything in the stores to buy, and choice of style or colour was nonexistent. One year, my entire class wore identical cowhide sandals, because that was the only available style in the stores.

If something better than average quality did show up in a store, the clerks phoned their family and friends to come buy it. This was how I got a smart-looking raincoat one year. My friend Marilla's father was the manager in a sporting goods store. He alerted my mother whenever something good came in and saved it until she could get there to buy it. Everything was in short supply, and everyone looked out for items their friends and family needed. Home-based seamstresses and knitters did a brisk business creating unique items that set the wearer a little apart, or filled a need the government-run stores couldn't meet.

The materials these craftspeople needed were also hard to find, so a whole network of black market dealing grew, with go-betweens to match people who received a parcel of wool from, say, Australia, with knitters who had clients wanting a sweater.

Sometimes the client brought her own wool, received in a parcel or swapped for something else with another recipient of a gift from the west. My mother was such a go-between with nylons. A Swiss diplomat brought in nylons whenever he went home, and Mother sold his wares for a commission to her stocking-mending clients. Someone else placed a few bottles of nail polish with her on consignment and it sold well. When a friend needed a specific medication for high blood pressure, Mother approached the Swiss diplomat and he brought the medicine on his next trip.

Because of the general craving for something a little smarter or nicer, the silk kerchiefs my mother and her friend Mariska painted sold well. Those who could afford to do so custom-ordered a pattern and color. The next level chose carefully from the ready-made but handcrafted kerchiefs, and the poorest bought factory-printed silk imitation ones from stores. In Budapest, they rarely wore cotton or wool, except for country people, old women or children. Old "grandes dames" like my grandmother would never give up their hats, communism or not. My clever grandmother altered her hat every spring by giving it a punch with her small fist and stitching the new crease in place. A colourful scarf and —sometimes— new buttons on her dress completed her stylish spring wardrobe. All foreign-made clothing items were hot sellers. Among my peers, roll-top pencil cases, red elastic belts, pop-together plastic beads and ballpoint pens were on everyone's wish list.

Government officials wouldn't handle routine requests, like giving out a tax certificate, until the infamous "envelope," containing a sum of money, slipped into their hands. However, if the contribution were big enough, they'd bend or break the rules to satisfy the needs of the donor. If there was no envelope, the bureaucrat might deny or interminably delay a routine stamp. Doctors would give only basic care without the envelope, reserving their time and effort for those who could "show their gratitude." Being a nosy sort of child who stored snippets of information as a hobby, I listened in on many conversations of adults debating how much money they should place in the "envelope" to satisfy the recipient.

People already reduced to bare subsistence wages had to find a way to get the funds to fill those envelopes. Those who were well off before the war could sell a painting, some china or jewellery to the government-run second-hand shop to finance the gratuity. Long line-ups at the buying window of those shops attested to the number of people who needed to sell their keepsakes just to survive. Old ladies hauled out the family tea set, or elderly gentlemen showed a gold pocket watch inscribed "for long and loyal service." They waited anxiously to see if the evaluator offered enough to cover the latest family crisis. War medals, furniture, rare books, Oriental carpets and tiaras found their way to the second-hand dealers. Since market demand for these valuables was low —only the new upper echelon could afford to collect nice things— the prices offered were also very low.

The central pawnshop was equally busy. Those who thought a temporary loan would bridge them over a difficult time lined up all day with their goods to get the needed cash. For smaller problems, they borrowed from friends.

My mother had a childhood friend, Klári, who worked as a stenographer. Klári was a widow, trying hard to raise her athletic teenage son Gábor. Her wages couldn't cover the bare necessities to feed them. Klári didn't have much to sell or hock. Her family wasn't wealthy. Her husband had made a decent living as some minor business employee, but not much beyond that. They didn't have much opportunity to collect antiques, Oriental rugs or other valuable home furnishings. Her home was modern, bright and airy and I remember it as the cleanest place, without it feeling antiseptic, that I ever saw. They didn't live far from us and we dropped in often for a brief visit.

A generous cousin in Chicago supplemented Klári's funds regularly, but because the money came through a black-market channel, it was sometimes late. She had to borrow grocery money from my mother. As often as not, my mother, in turn, was short, and had to hock a piece of jewellery to bridge the gap. I saw very little of Gábor, but have very warm memories of him treating me like a little sister. Gábor worked out, kayaking, every spare moment he had and his most fervent wish was to become a doctor. When he wasn't on the water, he was holed up in his tiny room, preparing for his entrance exams for medical school.

His chances of getting into medical school were slim to none, but he plodded along, trying his best to get high marks to balance his social stigma. There were strict quotas on who could get into University. The distribution pattern was as follows: over fifty percent of the student body had to come from the proletariat or blue-collar families, thirty-five percent from peasant families, ten percent from the intelligentsia, and only five percent from the ranks of the former "exploiting" classes classified as "other.

As predicted, he didn't make it on his first try and got a job as a porter in a hospital in hopes of earning points for being a labourer toward his next application. The work was arduous, often boring and only paid a pittance, but he loved it because it got him close to medicine. Two years later, he finally gained acceptance as a mature student with medical experience. He became a neurologist. Most likely, he cultivated the friendship of one or two physicians at the hospital and thereby gained some connections to the Medical School.

In order to have enough students to fill the spaces reserved for the proletariat and peasant classes, they designed a special program for older students, twenty to twenty-five year olds, who only had a grade eight education, sometimes even less, but who were communist party members or had the desired background. They prepared these individuals in special schools for matriculation in one year, instead of the four years required for high school. Usually, they only took subjects necessary for their further education, in order to continue in their specialized studies. In addition, these persons didn't have to take an entrance exam. They had guaranteed acceptance by virtue of their social status. Some of them, because of their acceleration, were barely literate, but, of course, the professors were too scared to fail them. They sailed through the program and became mediocre professionals in the high government positions guaranteed by their social rank.

Some faculties were more difficult to get into than others. Agriculture wasn't very popular; therefore, if I cultivated the connections gained in my summer job at the School of Horticulture, and perhaps worked for a year or two in the school at some menial job, I could become a student there.

Connections were very important in all facets of life. It was truly a society where who you knew was more important than what you knew. Everyone was networking, making contact with the grand niece of the neighbour's aunt to get a privilege.

———

The bourgeoisie label haunted even the professionals, since the party presumed their families must have been well off in former days to have been able to send them to University. Doctors were a minor exception to this rule. While they too worked, regimented, in government-controlled clinics with fixed salaries, no one could keep the grateful patients from showing their appreciation with a gift of money or a fresh chicken. An entire underground economy based on gratuity developed, and it haunts Hungary's economy to this day.

Revolution

Luli

Jóska Junior, nicknamed Luli, my mother's cousin, took an interest in my welfare when I was in my early teens. We met, just the two of us, in fabulous pastry shops. He bought me whatever I wanted, often chastising me for not choosing a fancier, more expensive concoction. In selecting my treat, I couldn't help myself. I liked simple things and didn't get excited by towers of whipped cream which, generously, he would have liked me to pick. I loved being with Luli. Since he never had a child, he treated me as if I were an adult and, of course, this was special and flattering to a thirteen year old. I could talk to him and be sure of his full attention, yet he had me giggling frequently when he twisted words around to be funny.

Luli was a professor of architecture at the University. He was well respected for his knowledge and publications in his field, which resulted in higher than average earnings without having to become embroiled in politics to keep his job. I adored him. I'd had a deep interest in architecture ever since I could read. There were numerous illustrated books on architecture in our home, books my Uncle Róbert left behind when he left Hungary in 1939. I pored over these books and even learned to read the captions in German in one of the large folios about the Bauhaus design, diligently looking up the words in a dictionary. Two of my grandmother's brothers were architects of some renown --one of them Luli's father-- and on our walks, my grandmother pointed proudly to buildings her brothers created. Her own son, my Uncle Róbert, had studied in Vienna and fled Hungary just as the Second World War broke out. For a few months, he lived in the émigré enclave of Paris, but as the war spread, he made his way to Spain where the Civil War had just ended and the need for architects to reconstruct offered an opportunity to rebuild his own life.

Luli also became an architect, but took the tangential route in his career of becoming an art historian specializing in the archaeology of architecture. His special interest was in research leading to the restoration of historic buildings. Since Budapest lay in ruins after the war, the need for his expertise was great. The damage to the buildings exposed former styles hidden under modernization efforts. In rebuilding, he considered elements of the original architecture. Digging through the rubble, the style changes revealed themselves; he studied the age and the history of the building and then created a detailed plan of reconstruction using as many of the salvageable elements as possible. He augmented the work with newly-carved pieces to successfully solve these giant three-dimensional puzzles. The subject fascinated me, and I listened with rapt attention as he explained his work.

In grade school, we took a bit of art history as part of the Art curriculum, and I had the opportunity to join an extracurricular history of art club in high school. I worked hard to learn about the history of architecture. On weekends, I dragged my mother to ruins to examine and touch the stones holding the mysteries of past centuries. She complained continuously during these outings, exclaiming: "If you've seen one ruin, you've seen them all!" I explained patiently the differences as I had learnt in my art history club. Mother tried to channel me into activities that weren't so boring for her, like visiting friends and relatives, but nothing could deter me. I loved those stones. They spoke to me about history and craftsmanship and, to me, they were alive and exciting. With Luli, I was in heaven. I asked him to explain or elaborate on what I'd read about in art history, while sitting across the table from him in one of those wonderful pastry shops that smelled of vanilla, chocolate and steaming coffee.

The house-to-house battle of Budapest in the spring of 1945 devastated the historic Castle Hill district. The Germans holed up for weeks in the secret underground passages of the plateau on which the Royal Castle, government offices and homes of courtiers once sat. The plateau, with the Buda Hills as a green backdrop, rose sharply out of the surrounding flats and overlooked the slowly meandering Danube. It was the most scenic symbol of the city, as well as the historic reason for Buda's existence. Even the Romans, before the Hungarians conquered the land, realized the value of the plateau, which provided a clear view of the advancing and limited approaches to the sheer cliffs, while the Danube below provided water and easy transport of goods. Hardly a building was left standing in the district in 1945. Rubble littered the ancient cobblestones; a carved cornice here, a sightless frame of a gothic window there, the once-invincible Romanesque doors on top of the heap. Craters in the pavement attested to the fierce fighting. Gaping buildings displayed their twisted pipes, and stood crumbling as silent witnesses to the devastation. Bullet holes pockmarked the Fisherman's Bastion, a whimsical structure built at the turn of the twentieth century to commemorate Hungary becoming home to the Magyars a thousand years before. The plans for reconstruction started soon after the war, but actual work had to wait until funds could be spared and manpower provided from the repair of essential housing and industries.

The first reconstruction project was the repair of the badly damaged Mátyás Church, Hungary's coronation church, overlooking Pest from the plateau. The church was an important historical site, a symbol of Budapest's skyline, and its restoration was a confident message to the people that the war was over. This monumental task was Luli's life work. He studied the history of the building reaching back to the thirteenth century, and planned the minute details he needed to resurrect the wonder of this architectural masterpiece.

Luli was a generous man. He knew my mother had a hard time making ends meet, so he took it upon himself to order a handmade pair of shoes for me at an elegant boutique in the most fashionable Belváros district. I could choose whatever style I wanted, he told the shoemaker, as the latter bent over my foot to take measurements. I chose cream-colored leather with thick crepe rubber soles, in a moccasin style. I admired these on other people, but knew deep in my heart that even dreaming about them was impractical. We didn't have that kind of money.

The day the shoes were to be ready, I primped for hours to make sure my appearance matched the importance of the occasion. Foolishly, I decided that, in spite of the icy wind, nothing short of my best nylons suited this event. Greeting my new possession just couldn't be done in sensible cotton stockings. As I waited for the streetcar, the cold numbed my shins and they were red and raw by the time I got to the shoemaker's to meet Luli, but I never uttered a word of complaint. To this day, my shins are red, itchy and shiny in winter, a souvenir of freezing the skin on that memorable afternoon long ago.

There are days in everyone's life that start off as ordinary, but turn out so magically, that recalling them sends a warm glow to one's eyes, even decades later. One of those days happened on September 30, 1956. Luli was taking me on an outing to the village of Szentendre. Since we seldom ventured out of the city except for vacations, I was quite unfamiliar with this charming village hugging the Danube, just a few kilometres north of Budapest.

I met Luli and his charismatic young assistant, Erzsike, at the appointed time at the train station. While the sun was still warm, the air already had a bit of an autumn nip to it in the early morning. A quick introduction to Erzsike and we were on our way to Szentendre in the rattling train. Erzsike matched the morning perfectly. Her fresh face was rimmed in a halo of blond curls and her laughing eyes were as open and honest as the unvarnished early autumn air. The three of us chatted amicably on the train until we got to Szentendre about an hour later. The town was like a place forgotten in time.

War seemed to have skipped this little spot of Hungary. Horse-drawn carriages meandered down the cobbled street, undisturbed by the internal combustion engines of the city. Because it was Sunday, few people were on the street. At the tiny roadside chapel, two old ladies in country attire, their heads covered with black kerchiefs, gossiped in a strange language. I soon found out they were speaking Serbian.

Serbs populated this town in the late 1600s, when the Turkish invasion pushed north seven fleeing families in fear of persecution from different parts of the Balkans. They settled in this village and started a new life. Since the seven Serb founding groups couldn't agree on building a church together to practice their orthodox faith, they each built a church of their own. Consequently, this small settlement boasted seven orthodox churches and one Roman Catholic, which stood at the top of the largest hill.

As we wove our way through the narrow streets and alleys, every vista was a new and exciting experience for me. The buildings were fascinating. The heavily carved doors and windows were each a separate work of art. Wrought iron decorations, arches, and carved stone had me whipping my head back and forth, drinking in the architectural charm of the place. Climbing a narrow, steep alley, we were suddenly in a large walled garden where ancient trees cast shade on the grass. From the parapet of the wall, which overlooked the tiled rooftops of the town, we saw the seven other churches and the Danube with its pebbled shore in the distance. The Catholic Church stood between the trees. Its plainness was something of an anticlimax. The ochre-plastered walls and the shape of the bell tower made it look like any other baroque church in rural Hungary. As we wandered around the building, Luli examined the structure with an expert's concentration and commented to Erzsike from time to time. When we arrived at the heavy timber side door, he became quite excited at the sight of the peeling plaster. As he later explained, plaster and the coats of paint it revealed were important markers in dating the renovations done to a building. There was a faint line in the plaster at about shoulder level just to the right of the door, and he scratched the spot with his key ever so gently, but I sensed his growing excitement. When he finished, a cross about two inches long painted on one of the earlier layers of plaster became clearly visible. It was a small, primitive mark, but a great clue and useful in establishing the date of the plaster layer. Luli and Erzsike discussed their find at length while I drank in the pure air and the beauty of the place. Though the conversation centered on their work, I sensed a bond of intimacy between them. Luli was recently divorced, and it didn't take much intuition to realize there was a very special relationship between him and Erzsike. It was the kind of happy and comfortable intimacy that included everything and everyone around them, even me. Leisurely, we made our way back to the central square to have our lunch, a delicious authentic Serb meal of spicy meat and rice, in one of the restaurants.

After that, we headed out to the bank of the Danube for a stroll along the gently-curving tree-lined promenade. The row of houses as we left the town centre became more and more like small castles. Each sat in a large park-like setting with curved carriage drives leading to an elegant front entrance. The villas were no longer new, the cherubs holding up the wrought iron balconies were missing a few body parts, the gardens were overgrown with neglect, but even in their decline, they looked like dowagers, stately and serene. Luli pushed open the great garden gate of one of these grand houses and we followed him along the broken pavement to a small back entrance, where an elderly lady answered his knock on the door. She was dignified, but her once- elegant attire was threadbare. As soon as she recognized her visitor, her wrinkled face dissolved into a smile of pure pleasure. She was happy to have us visit her, but quite upset she didn't even have tea to offer us. She lived in a single room stuffed with furniture, paintings, oriental rugs, bric-a-brac that looked valuable, and a rusting iron stove in one corner for heating. The room felt dark and damp, even on this beautiful Indian summer day. The paint on the walls peeled and rosettes of salt leached from the bricks. She had no water or toilet in the room. She had to carry water from a tap around the corner, and she used the outhouse at the end of the garden. Erzsike and I sat in silence while Luli inquired about the old lady's health and asked her how she managed. She tried to be upbeat, but anyone could see her survival hung by a thread. She hugged each of us in turn as we said goodbye. Luli bent to kiss her hand and I saw him slip a large bill into her palm quickly. Her other hand shot up as if to object, but Luli quickly closed her fist around the currency and said, "I insist!" Tears welled in her eyes and speechlessly, she waved from the doorway as we left. In silence, each of us wrapped in the poignant impressions of the past hour, we headed back toward the town.

At the end of the promenade, Luli herded us into a café,

The Greek Ewer, and ordered Turkish coffee for the three of us. There in the semi-darkness, sitting on low stools, I had my first cup of real coffee and listened to the story of the old lady we'd just met. Her deceased husband had been a prominent architect whose works included some of Budapest's most famous landmarks. The villa was theirs, and she had entertained the cream of Budapest society and the celebrated members of the Szentendre artist community with the help of a staff of servants. After the communists came to power, she was declared bourgeois, a distrusted "enemy of the state," and forced to give up her house to a high communist party official as his residence. She was fortunate to have secured the former storage room in the back as living quarters for herself. Since she had neither a pension nor any other regular income, she eked out a living selling some of the valuables seen around her room that she had salvaged from her splendid home.

While the story was sad, we all felt happy about having brightened the old lady's day. We boarded the train for home in high spirits. Luli promptly fell asleep from the gentle swinging of the car while Ezsike and I talked, getting to know each other better. By the time the train pulled into the station, we were fast friends, the age difference of eight or nine years having evaporated. We had built a lifelong bond.

Of course, when I got home, the rest of the family quizzed me thoroughly about Luli's new lady friend. I was the center of attention, because as it turned out, everyone else had to wait a couple of weeks to meet Erzsike in person.

Three weeks later, the revolution broke out and in six short weeks, my life was turned upside down. Luli came to the rescue again when we decided to escape from Hungary. He provided the ready cash to pay for the guides necessary for such an undertaking, and assured us he'd market the contents of our apartment carefully and use the funds to provide for my grandmother for the rest of her life. A promise he kept.

———

Budapest is three cities: Buda, Óbuda, and Pest, which joined in 1873 to form the city of Budapest. Bit by bit, small towns on the outskirts have joined the unified city, which now has twenty-three districts and a population of over a million. Buda was the historical capital, centered on the imperial castle. It has been occupied for centuries and one could recognize samples of almost all the major styles of the civilized world in its architecture. The castle was built on a small plateau overlooking the river for easy defence. The houses of nobles, high officials, and some government offices were located on the plateau before the war. During the siege of Budapest, the fighting was so fierce in this district that the entire district was a mass of rubble after the war. Repair and reconstruction didn't start until the fifties. The streets were pockmarked, broken stone was everywhere and buildings were left with one wall pointing skyward amidst the pile of ruins. From time to time, an unexploded bomb went off in one of the ruins and maimed the children who found it in their quest for scrap metal. Due to the acute metal shortage, we were always asked to search for scrap metal and turn it into the local recycling depot for cash. Some children got so enthusiastic that they turned in the brass knobs from their parent's beds. Others, like my husband and his friend, prowled the ruins to salvage the lead pipes for some extra pocket money without realizing the danger from bombs and collapsing walls.

Luli lived a short but happy life married to Erzsike. He died young, at fifty-four, of a chronic ailment he contracted during the war.

I feel Luli's presence in the Mátyás Church. There I sit in awe of his masterpiece in one of the oak pews, caressing every curve, every arch with my eyes. The streaming tourists around me with their exclamations of wonder fill me with pride. I'd love to shout to them, "You should have met this remarkable man!" However, of course I keep quiet. His memory is my special treasure. I visit the church and Szentendre on every visit to Hungary. At every opportunity I have, I see Erzsike, a well-known professor of architecture and a globe-trotting, effervescent personality. Invariably, we recall that very special happy day in Szentendre so long ago.

October 23, 1956

Our concerns in 1956 centred on where would we find a piece of meat, how long would the line-up for eggs be, or would there be bologna to buy for today's supper? Where will we find the money to buy a new pair of shoes or a new blouse? The stores were usually empty. Most people had shut out politics, from thought and conversation, long ago. What was the point in dealing with illogical, unalterable and depressing? In high school, we had a subject called Ideology, when we had to show our political awareness of the communist system.

I was fifteen and in second year at the Kossuth Zsuzsanna High School. The school and especially the principal, Mrs. Otta, were infamous for its strict adherence to the communist doctrine. Anyone she thought was less than totally committed to the political system quickly disappeared, from our ranks, expelled. Everyone was a potential informer, from friends to teachers and even the custodian. Part of the survival mode was to get the daily communist youth newspaper and spew it back with conviction in the Ideology class. Mrs. Otta sat in the back in her steel-grey satin smock and we felt her piercing eyes cut through our facade.

I had a great advantage in being able to keep up with current affairs. The paper usually ran out by six in the morning at the news stands. However, my former wet-nurse was a rikkancs, a street newsvendor, one of those poor women dressed in rags shivering on the street corners, screaming out the daily headlines to sell papers. Ever since I could remember, I stopped to say hello when I passed her and she always greeted me with visible pleasure. Her tired face lit up at the sight of me. She felt I was part of her, through her milk, and she was proud of me. So when I took my problem to her, she was happy to oblige. When the paper arrived at four a.m., she tucked the first copy under the tattered cushion of her chair for Évike, me, to pick up at the civilized hour of seven. Although I read the paper religiously at breakfast and successfully spewed back what was expected, I never bothered to digest the contents. It was safer that way. Those who read critically always got into trouble, because their individual opinion always crept into their presentations and provided Mrs. Otta fodder for a tirade. Being careful not to interpret the news was just part of what you had to do to survive, like washing and dressing.

I was so busy concentrating on staying out of trouble that the political events that started in early 1956 just went past me. I had no friends in school except for Vera, a statuesque redhead who answered my call of, "Who goes toward the number six streetcar?" early in first year. Vera was in another class, but we usually waited for each other on the steps to walk home together. Without any previous dialogue, we had an understanding to avoid all dangerous subjects. I knew what street she lived on and that she had to pass our house to go home, but had no idea what her parents did for a living or even if she had siblings. I was never invited to her home, and she never came to mine. She was an accomplished violinist and talked about her lessons and recitals — a safe subject. Once, she invited me to accompany her to a concert where she was performing a solo piece. I was glad to go and as we trudged along in the fog to the distant auditorium, I wondered why someone from her family didn't go with her. I was her lone groupie, holding onto her coat, checking her hair and calming her nerves as she prepared. The auditorium was full, mostly with parents and relatives of the young musicians, a very appreciative audience. On the streetcar heading home, Vera thanked me for coming with her and for the support I gave her. When we got to our stop, she shook my hand, the customary Hungarian farewell, and we headed home in opposite directions.

I was determined to stay out of trouble and even when a co-worker, another summer student, tried to explain what was going on in politics, I changed the subject. I had enough problems without touching politics. Due to my success in my summer job, which resulted in the principal relaxing her iron grip on me, I almost liked going to school. I still kept my distance from most of my classmates, but I was no longer paranoid about whom I walked with going to school or returning home. Eszter, a very gregarious classmate, passed my house every day and if her streetcar were early, she showed up without invitation as I was having breakfast, to walk to school with me. She lived in a distant suburb of Óbuda and my home was just four blocks from the school.

Tuesday, October 23, 1956 was another fine fall day, warm for late October. When I arrived in class, an unusual sight greeted me. The normally quiet classroom was abuzz and someone waved a newspaper. I hadn't got one that morning, because we didn't have Ideology class and I'd gotten a bit lax about reading every word of the paper, since Mrs. Otta had stopped watching me like a hawk. Someone read the fifteen-point demands of the University students. Everyone, even those who walked in the shadows like me, commented on these demands. I was still too scared to really become part of the discussion and too ignorant because of my policy not to absorb the political news, so I stayed on the fringe of the excited group. What was most unusual was the math teacher, normally severe and unyielding in discipline, walked into the class and mildly requested us to calm down and take our seats. On normal days, one look from her froze our blood and sent us scurrying to our desks, but this time she didn't seem to care if we obeyed her request or not. All the teachers were more mellow and undemanding. At recess, small groups formed to further discuss politics, but I managed, without being obvious, to busy myself with other things to avoid being in such a dangerous crowd. I was distrustful and still in survival mode. After school, I walked home with Vera, my safe friend. We talked about her upcoming music recital, the weather, and homework, avoiding the topics of the day. That was the last time I saw Vera.

As usual, after dropping off my books, I went to have my meal at the nearby Tej Büfé. The restaurant served cheap meals, cafeteria-style, based on milk products. The food was reasonably good, inexpensive and substantial. On the way back, if I had a few forints left from the meal, I went into the music store and bought the printed sheets with words to one of the latest hits on the radio.

These cheap, small sheets of printed paper were one of the few luxuries I allowed myself. I gave the other stores a pass, except for the florist where I always stopped to admire the displays in the window.

Once home, I turned on the radio to the popular music request program where the "decadent" Western song of the forties, such as "Moulin Rouge" or "Autumn Leaves, "played among the Hungarian hits of the day. With the music in the background, I made myself comfortable at the wide windowsill that served as my desk and started my homework. It was a beautiful late Indian summer day, but too chilly to leave the window open. At three o'clock, a telephone call shook me out of my cocoon. My mother called from work. By that time, she had joined a crafter's cooperative and had a spot in a notions store — about three streetcar stops from our home— where she sat and repaired stockings. Student demonstrations stopped the streetcars on the Körút, the main boulevard of Budapest. Mother was experienced at sensing the peaceful demonstration would soon escalate. She remembered the red terror after World War I, the white terror that followed, not to mention the Second World War. "When trouble starts, you have to have food!" she announced. She perceived trouble. She told me she was going to carry her heavy stocking repair machine home through the quiet back streets. I was to stay put, gather all the money I could find, and be ready to go grocery shopping when she arrived home.

Mother had a unique budgeting system in the linen cabinet. The rent was between the folds of her special pink bedding, food money was layered between the tablecloths, money for clothing was among the dishtowels, and so forth. We were so badly off at this point that we didn't have a morsel of extra food in the house to fall back on. We lived day-to-day. At times, we returned the milk bottles for the deposit money to buy something to eat.

Having gathered the money, I went to the lobby of our apartment building, which was already filled with a dozen neighbours milling about, peeking out at the Körút, a block away, to see the demonstrations and discuss the events. Here, the conversation was quite relaxed. We didn't have to worry about being politically correct. Most of these people had moved into the thirty-six-unit building when it was new in 1935. They were similar in social status, had lived through the war together, coped with nationalizations, food shortages and communism side by side, making the best of the bad.

Bit by bit, other tenants returning home joined the group, bringing morsels of about demonstrations in other parts of the city. One of them looked at us and asked if we were gathered to see "The Thief of Baghdad," a movie that played to sold-out audiences at the time. Laughter followed his ironic comment. From my vantage point, I saw the crowd of disciplined, but shouting students with signs pass our street. The crowd roared when the Hungarian flag, with a hole cut out to rid it of the hated communist emblem of the hammer and sickle, went up on the corner building across the boulevard.

When Mother got home, we went grocery shopping. We spent every forint I had gathered earlier on bread, butter, bologna and milk. The money didn't go far, and I didn't dare ask my mother where we were going to get the money for rent or electricity later. Night fell as we finished gathering what foodstuffs we could. In the meantime, the crowd continued to head toward the bridge in a steady stream, about twenty abreast, as if all of Budapest was on the move with a single goal. Older people joined the demonstration, and then trucks loaded with factory workers from the industrial suburbs showed up. As we stood on the sidewalk watching, Mother pointed to a man who stood on the corner with a plate of food, eating and watching. He obviously came out of the self-serve restaurant and was oblivious to how he looked to others. Mother said, "Tonight is history in the making, and you'll remember that man as long as you live." She was right.

At home, a flooding toilet greeted us. Ours was the bottom toilet on the stack, where six stories of apartments were emptying into the plugged sewer. Mother started to clean it up and I ran to ask all the tenants above to stop using their toilets. Of course, in the anonymity of six suites, some did continue to flush and the water kept coming. There was no one to fix the problem. Tati, our master of all trades, had died just a few weeks before, when he left the gas unlit on his kitchen stove.

Luckily, Hungarian architects foresaw such a disaster and had put a half-inch ledge between the rooms, so as long as we kept cleaning, the rest of the apartment wasn't in danger of being flooded with the stinking water. Rags took too long, so Mother started to use the dustpan to shovel the water into the pail. When the pail was full, I carried it outside and poured the contents over the rail into the courtyard. After a while, bits of glossy paper started to come out with the water, the obvious the cause of the calamity. Someone above us probably had some documents they were afraid to possess and flushed the torn pieces down the toilet. We shovelled and poured for uncounted hours. We were near exhaustion when a couple of strong arms shoved us aside and took over.

While we were working, the army billeted into the building a platoon of Hungarian soldiers, very young recruits, to prevent snipers from entering. By that time, as we found out later, the secret police was shooting into the crowds of demonstrators at the radio station and the workers from the industrial suburb of Csepel had toppled the Stalin statue and dragged it to the National Theatre a couple of kilometres away. Some of the soldiers from the barracks in Budapest had joined the demonstrators and supplied them with weapons. The armed demonstrators had commandeered windows and were shooting back at the authorities. Our building was in a strategic location. We were only six blocks from the Parliament, two blocks from the Ministry of Defence, three blocks from the mint and one block from the courts and the city jail. When asked which side they were on, our platoon answered, "On yours. We're here to keep snipers out. If they start shooting out from this building, you're in danger, because someone will shoot back."

The soldiers sealed off the building for the next two weeks and everyone had to show their identity booklets coming and going. Tenants had to vouch for their visitors, their names and the hosts were recorded, and they had to be out by a given time. Most of the time, during the day, a little group of tenants congregated about at the entrance, peeking out to see what was happening and exchanging news of the events. When not in the lobby, we listened to the radio. The first few days were euphoric; the revolution was succeeding and the population behaved in exemplary fashion, not touching the goods in the broken store windows and collecting money in unmanned boxes throughout the city to help the cause.

Sometime during those first few days, I don't know if it was due to the frantic toilet cleaning effort or fear, but I became very ill. My always-fragile stomach tied itself into a painful knot and I couldn't hold down any food. Two days of starvation left me too weak to move and as I lay on the sofa, only the open front door threw a narrow sheaf of light into the dark, windowless living room. A figure appeared in the doorway and came to kneel beside me. I couldn't see his face, but he gently lifted my head, held a glass to my lips, and told me to drink it all up. It was vile stuff. I'd had little sips of alcohol before, but this harsh, stinky brew took my breath away. The soldier holding the glass patted me on the head and told me to stay put. As if I could move. In addition to feeling utterly exhausted, now the room was spinning. He returned minutes later with an aluminium bowl and fed me slowly with a spoon. The soldier's ration was quite awful, congealed greasy rice with bits of grisly meat, but I didn't want to hurt his feelings, so I bravely forced it down. Miraculously, the rough brandy relaxed my stomach enough that I could hold this nourishing, albeit horrible food. I never found out which of the platoon members came to administer his first alcohol ration and then fed me, but soon I was up and well.

Things seemed calm. Mother and I ventured out for a short walk. There were all kinds of notices on the walls posted by the new government of Imre Nagy. They printed several newspapers, too, and distributed them free to the news-hungry population. People talked of their views without restraint on street corners. Nobody had to look over his or her shoulder to see who was listening. We heard there was still fighting in some areas of the city, but those places were relatively far from us, so we enjoyed the late Indian summer and the general exhilaration of our neighbourhood.

It never occurred to me to write Vera from Canada or to locate her on my subsequent visits to Budapest. What could I say to her? It wasn't a real friendship. Yet for over a year, we were faithful companions.

Eva in High School uniform, fall of 1956

When the Chips are down

As the days of the revolution wore on, people spent more
and more time in the lobby, cautiously peering out to the
boulevard where nothing much occurred. One tenant, a well-
known heart specialist, announced there was nothing to fear and
he would go to see what was happening beyond. As we watched,
he nonchalantly set off only to scurry back, white- faced, when a
metal roller blind somewhere sounded like the discharge of a gun.
The lobby group burst out laughing. Most of these people had
lived in the building for decades and knew each other well. They
had the normal trivial squabbles about radios playing too loudly
and shaking dusters right after the tenant below had washed the
balcony. Some of these fights even went as far as people never
speaking to each other again. They weren't heroes nor courageous,
but from time to time they rose to a greatness no one would have
suspected.

One of these occasions was in the early fifties, when the
three generations of the Kövi family were served notice to vacate
their treasure-laden apartments within twenty-four hours and were
banished to the country, because old Mr. Kövi used to be a
banker. The entire family —his ailing wife, his married daughter,
his son-in-law and even their three-year-old granddaughter,
Márta— had to pay for the crime of having been a successful man
before the war. When their orders came, the building became a
beehive of activity. The neighbours packed and stored the
valuables, the former maids of the various tenants, who were now
living in rented spare rooms throughout the building and eked out
a living as cleaning women on a daily rate, quickly made food for
the trip. The older children, like me, took care of little Márta, so
she didn't get in the way. In a memorable feat of cooperation,

people moved silently, as if they followed a well-rehearsed script, and the two apartments were empty in much less than the allotted twenty-four hours. It was a memorable feat of teamwork. Of course, no one had the courage to come out at dawn the next day to say goodbye when the Kövis left for their designated farm —on top of an army truck— to toil from morning till night digging potatoes and feeding the pigs. Mrs. Kövi died shortly after the ordeal began.

The Kövi's former maid Mari, a young farm girl, managed to request from the authorities one of the two vacated apartments and stayed behind living in it comma while the Kövis laboured on the farm, for re-education purposes, for the next two or three years. When they got permission to return shortly before the revolution, Mari returned their home to them and moved into the tiny maid's room of the apartment with her husband, Miki.

Miki was a shy, poor country boy, in his early twenties. He was always polite and helpful. He took heavy parcels from a tenant's hand and carried them to the door, quietly, expecting nothing in return but a thank you. He was a "nobody," a simple conscript in the despised and feared Államvédelmi Osztály, or ÁVO, the all-powerful secret police. When he was called for his mandatory military duty, he chose the ÁVO, probably for the promise of a bigger bowl of soup, just as so many others like him did.

We also had an ÁVO officer, Peter, a doctor, living in the building. When Peter and his family moved in, the tenants greeted him with suspicion, but as he became a familiar neighbour, his ÁVO uniform went almost unnoticed. His humanity, willingness to give of himself, and his charming wife and daughter made us blind to his ÁVO affiliation. Peter gave a helping hand when people were ill or just wanted to know if their own doctor had given them the right advice. They always could count on his wife to sympathize when someone needed a listener. The children liked and accepted their daughter, a gregarious ten-year-old. Although they were better off than most of the tenants, they took pains not to flaunt it.

The tenants particularly appreciated Peter when one of the

neighbours took seriously ill during the revolt and had to have a blood test to confirm the diagnosis. Peter's wife made her husband an armband of white cloth with a large red cross crudely painted on it. The radio announced doctors should wear such an armband and then they could flag down any vehicle and request assistance to get to their patients or hospitals. Short-sighted, Peter flagged down the first vehicle, which happened to be a Russian armoured car. He was scared, but the Russians took him to the hospital without a word. The tests done, Peter returned a few hours later with medication for his patient.

On the fifth day after the start of the uprising, a rag-tag group of revolutionary militia came to the apartment lobby. They wanted to know if there were any members of the ÁVO living in the building. Without hesitation, the dozen or more people in the lobby replied in indignant unison, "Of course not!"

The next day, Miki showed up to join the gawking group in the lobby. When we looked closely at his attire, we could identify Judge L.'s worn shoes, Mr. B.'s old sweater, and Dr. V.'s slightly frayed custom shirt. The poor innocent lad hadn't even owned a change of civilian clothes and had been cowering in his small room, knowing that if he went outside in his uniform, he could be executed on the spot.

An amazing example of true cooperation!

————

This is a true story, although I've changed some of the names to protect the privacy of the individuals. Canada became home to several of these cast-of characters. My mother and I escaped from Hungary in December of that year. Since I owned no suitable shoes for the trek, Peter's wife gave me a pair of hers. Peter and his family went to Montreal to start a new life. Their daughter became a physician. I saw Márta Kövi again in the Canadian immigration camp near Vienna in January 1957, where she greeted me with a great choking hug. Her family was headed to Eastern Canada to join relatives there. No one has heard from them since.

Piri Mama

Piroska, affectionately nicknamed Piri Mama, was the popular childless "matron" of the apartment building, in recognition of her affinity to all the building's children. Piri Mama had an extraordinary life.

The brilliant daughter of a world renowned scholar, she studied medicine at the Sorbonne in Paris in the 1920's, graduating from a nearly all-male class with honours. Although she was a fully qualified surgeon when she returned to Budapest, as a woman she couldn't find employment. She married a wealthy businessman and practiced cosmetology instead, keeping up with medicine by reading the current literature in three languages. Her husband died just before the war. When the communist regime took over in Hungary, declaring equality for all, she seized the opportunity and applied for a position as a surgeon in one of the major hospitals of Budapest. Her medical and people skills resulted in rapid advancement. Without joining the party or participating in any political activity, she quickly rose to Chief of Surgery in her hospital. It was as if the pent-up years of waiting for her opportunity propelled her. Her only concession to the regime was that she wore a kerchief on her head and the uniform-like green wool loden overcoat of the masses. She didn't want to cause trouble. Even dressed like that, she had an aura of elegance. Her dyed blonde hair, dressed meticulously in a fashionable large chignon, and her confident bearing made her stand out in a crowd as a personality. She looked the fulfilled, confident professional. In private life, she remained Piri Mama to all of us, warm and caring, but just a little bit larger than life.

Miraculously, it looked as if this courageous uprising of ordinary people, infuriated by the restrictive practices of the communist regime, might win. There were encouraging signs. Much of the Hungarian Army had sided with the rebels, or at least refused to shoot at the civilians. Radio Free Europe announced that U.S. troops were amassed on the Austrian border, ready to move in to aid the revolutionaries, comprised of students and factory workers armed with nothing more than Molotov cocktails and a few stolen guns. The Russian troops had withdrawn from the city. It seemed the impossible could happen and the brave Hungarians could chase the mighty Russians back to the other side of the Carpathian Mountains.

Cautious optimism prevailed. The teenaged boys of our apartment building ventured out to the suburban farms in search of food. The middle-aged tenants were more guarded. They only dared to go out to the boulevard to assess the damage, and soon came scurrying back to report their findings to the others congregated in the lobby. The great city was at a standstill. Only essential services functioned, which meant of the one hundred or so souls in the building, only three had to go to work. They were physicians, who under the emergency measures had the right to flag down any vehicle and demand to be taken to their respective hospitals.

The pack congregating in the lobby became thinner. Some even went back to doing normal tasks such as cleaning their homes. Being a nosy fifteen–year–old who enjoyed the loving attention of most of the tenants, I hung around the lobby, listening to the amateur political analysts.

On a bright, sunlit day about five days after the beginning of the Hungarian Revolution, all eyes were suddenly on the grand staircase leading down from the main landing of our apartment building. A vision such as we hadn't seen in years descended: Piri Mama, in a loud black-and-white hound's tooth suit with a mink boa wrapped around her shoulders and clasped head to tail on her ample bosom. A slightly dated hat perched on her head, and an alligator-skin purse completed her outfit. She looked like something out of a pre-war fashion magazine. On her sleeve, she wore a homemade white armband with a red cross crudely painted in red nail polish. A collective gasp rose from the crowd. Someone asked her gently if it were wise to venture out looking like that in the middle of a revolution.

She held her head high, shoulders erect, and replied, "I've have had enough of the dowdy kerchiefs and ubiquitous green loden coats. This is my way of celebrating the triumph of the revolution." With that parting shot, she was off, walking confidently toward the boulevard to flag down a passing military truck to take her to work.

A few days later, on Sunday, November fourth, at dawn, we awoke to the sounds of heavy shelling. The Russians were back with a vengeance. Tanks surrounded the city; the sky was ablaze. The promised American help was nowhere to be seen. We cowered in our apartments like beaten dogs. The lobby was empty. For several days, the shelling went on, then stopped abruptly. We slowly ventured out to the boulevard to find rubble everywhere. The city was, once more, in ruins, its spirit broken.

Piri Mama scurried down the street in her green loden coat, a faded kerchief on her head, medical bag in hand, and the armband on her sleeve to flag down a Russian vehicle to take her to her job.

———

In 1973, Leslie, my five-year old son, and I were walking down the street where I had spent my childhood. The familiar buildings and smells gripped my emotions and fragments of memories played hide-and-seek in my brain. Suddenly, my little son tripped and fell on the uneven pavement and scraped his knee. At the sight of blood, he wailed plaintively, but I assured him that as soon as we got to Piri Mama's, she'd take care of his "owie.".

Piri Mama opened the door to us with her familiar smile and assured Leslie he'd have immediate expert care for his wound. She took his little hands in hers and led him to her kitchen. He looked at her suspiciously as she opened a drawer and took out a bottle of disinfectant, scissors and gauze. All he had expected was a band-aid for his knee. She gently cleaned the scrape and proceeded to wrap the knee with gauze. I saw the distrust vanish in his eyes. "This old lady seems to know what she's doing," he thought.

Piri Mama was in her late-seventies then. She didn't get out much, but had a definite routine: reading books in German in the morning, Hungarian newspapers and magazines in the afternoon, and French tomes in the evenings. She didn't want her brain to go dead from disuse, she said, even though her body no longer obeyed her bidding.

The Outcome

"The first people who found themselves in the field against the Communist regime in Hungary were those whom that regime had pampered the most: writers, journalists, engineers, athletes, students, artists, and the like. Nine-tenths of those who started the demonstrations were students whose tuition and living expenses were paid by the government and who had been picked from the families of workers, peasants, and Communist Party officials. Yet they marched into the open to make their demands and then, when these were refused, stayed in the streets to fight. The first blood on the fateful evening of October 23 was shed by men of this kind." - Leslie B. Bain, "Hungary: The First Six Days," The Reporter, XV (November 15, 1956), 20-21.

A few days after the first demonstrations, euphoric optimism had followed. The battles at the radio station, near the barracks of Üllöi Street and elsewhere, became fiercer. The rebels erected barricades, snipers shot at the secret police, children battled tanks with Molotov cocktails, and the provisional government imposed a curfew to try to restore order. It looked as if the revolution could win and a new political order could take shape.

Although our segment of the city was relatively violence-free, partially because of the presence of the platoons of young soldiers billeted in the apartment buildings to keep snipers from occupying rooftops or windows, we heard the battles and shelling.

When the shelling was too intense or sounded too near, five or six of us bored teenagers in the building took to a windowless bathroom to play canasta for hours. We placed a board across the tub for a bench. One sat on the toilet lid, others on the ledge of the tub, and a kitchen stool was the table. It helped pass the time

in a helpless situation. About four days of this card- playing and
we were getting really hungry. People didn't have extra provisions
in those days. Therefore, when the shooting quieted down a bit,
the boys left on foot for the farming area on the outskirts of
Budapest to look for food. I'm not sure where they went, but all
they found to buy was a large sack of sunflower seeds. Since
things were relatively quiet, but still not safe to go out, we moved
the card game to our living room. We had a round table with a
little platform where the crossbars met. We poured the seeds into
a big bowl and placed the bowl on this platform. Everyone helped
himself and spat out the shells into the many ashtrays Mother
placed around the table.

Although we still cautiously congregated in the lobby, there
was little to be seen from our street, save for the thundering
vehicles going up and down the nearby boulevard. The Hungarian
radio gave conflicting reports as rebels alternated with the secret
police in controlling the broadcasts. The Voice of America and
Radio Free Europe, now free of interference, was our lifeline to
the events. Radio Free Europe even went so far as announcing
American troops were poised on the Austrian border, ready to
help the spirited rebels if they could continue their battle a little
longer. This lie encouraged hundreds of people to continue
fighting almost barehanded against the mighty Red Army.

Ugly rumours of summary executions of members of the
secret police, the ÁVO, reached us. A cousin of my mother's,
Pista, who had come to see if we were all right and to bring us
bread and butter, confirmed this. The food came just in time,
because our supplies had run out and we were forced to dampen
the dry bread crusts saved to feed our friends' pig to make "toast."
Pista was a political officer in the army and feared for his life. He
asked if he could stay with us, but Mother refused because she was
afraid of the repercussions. He accepted that, and went into hiding
at a friend's place in Buda.

On October 30th, the Russians withdrew from Budapest.
People walked the streets, talking freely about politics in small
groups without a care, unafraid of being overheard and punished.
Some people went to their offices, factories and schools and tore

down the photos of Lenin, Stalin and Rákosi who had looked down on us so fiercely, intimidating our spirits for so many years, and to cut holes in flags that still had the hammer and sickle emblem sewn on them.

My gregarious classmate Eszter showed up one day, having walked from distant Óbuda because public transportation was sporadic or non-existent. I was happy to see her well and welcomed her into our home. Apparently, from her description, Eszter's older brother had taken part in the fighting and her whole family was extremely proud of him. She asked me to come with her to help tear down the pictures in our school and make the principal, Mrs. Otta, cringe from a few well-chosen words. Much as my heart was with her, I was still leery of the reality of freedom and feared we'd both face retribution for such an action. I begged her to reconsider. Eszter was adamant that she had to go. I didn't seen her after that, but have often thought of her courage and hoped she and her family came to no harm by her actions.

The new government started to work. Cautious, disbelieving optimism filled the average citizen of Budapest until the eve of November 3rd, when the Prime Minister, Imre Nagy, announced Russian troops were gathered at Debrecen and he was negotiating their withdrawal. He and the Defence Minister, Pál Maléter, were summoned for "peace" talks to the Soviet Army Headquarters. That day, a male friend of one of our neighbours, who was a widow, missed the curfew and was stranded in the city. She felt having him stay would give rise to talk about her morals, so we moved into her apartment to guard her virtue. The male friend made his bed on the sofa in the living room, while the widow with Mother and I occupied the double bed in the minute apartment. A curtain separated the two rooms. At about four in the morning, we were shocked out of our slumber by the sound of heavy artillery. The sky was red with exploding shells. We stayed in bed, afraid to move. The gentleman from the living room, after every whistling hit, reassured us, "I was a gunner in the army during the war. From the sound of the booms, I can tell that these are outgoing shells, not incoming." We believed him because we wanted to believe him.

When daylight came, Budapest was in ruins once again and convoys of Soviet tanks rumbled down the boulevard. This was end of our short-lived freedom. An eerie quiet came over the city. Fear, disappointment and resignation hovered over hunched backs in the grey daylight. Friends greeted each other, but failed to stop for a chat. What was there to say? That the dreams of the last few weeks had been unrealistic? Every one knew that. No one could tell what the future held, and no one dared to think about it.

That night, a hysterical shriek brought the tenants to the gang. To our astonishment, Zsuzsi, a very private, mild-mannered and usually composed tenant, stood in front of her door in a white nightgown, screaming at the top of her lungs like a ghost. Her husband tried to quiet her, whispering soothing words to her. As she was getting ready for bed and went to close the curtains, she found herself looking down the muzzle of a Russian tank and panicked, resulting in this hysterical display. For several days, the gun pointed at her window and Zsuzsi, white-faced, slowly regained her composure. No one mentioned the incident; we all pretended not to have noticed her outburst because it would have embarrassed her.

Even when things started to become more normal —some of the public transportation was moving and most people went to work, at least for a brief period every day— there were incidents. My cousin arrived one day in the middle of the day, shaken and near panic. As she and many others were walking past the Ministry of Mining, a Russian tank, parked in the playground in front of the Ministry of Defence, opened fire on the building as she was walking toward our home. The shots went right over her head.

From one day to the next, the sky became grey and the weather tuned cold. Women seemed dowdier than ever and the idle chitchat on the street corners stopped. People went back into defensive mode. Thousands of people, for a variety of personal reasons, took to the road to freedom and decided to cross into Austria. My Mother and I were part of that group.

———

When I arrived in Canada, I didn't dare inquire after the fate of Eszter and her family, knowing that having a friend in the west meant yet another black mark against them and if they hadn't emigrated, it could add to their troubles.

The Tale of One Refugee

My mother and I arrived in Canada as refugees forty-five years ago. Our sudden journey to the unfamiliar began with a trip to a luggage shop to buy two small bags that would hold our most prized possessions. The Hungarian revolution of 1956 that had started with so much hope was quashed; Budapest was in ruins and bleeding. Mother yearned for the support and comfort of her brother, who had been living in Spain since the end of the Spanish Civil War. It made her set aside all her fears and phobias about being away from home for more than an hour or two, and she declared we were going. I was fifteen years old.

She hadn't made her decision lightly. The great migration started soon after the Russian tanks ended all hope on November 4th, 1956. Now, it was mid-December. We had spent the evenings of the past month glued to the radio, listening to Radio Free Europe broadcasting messages from friends and relatives who had safely made it to Austria.

Mother's best friend, Mariska, who was a decisive leader, her husband, Ödön and daughter Jutka were leaving, which gave Mother the courage to join in this trek to the unknown. It was decided the five of us would have to rent a hotel room near the railroad station the night before, so as not to be conspicuous in our neighbourhood leaving in the early morning, carrying our satchels.

We packed these small bags over and over again. Mother's heavy stocking repair machine had to go in first. After all, she had to make a living somehow, she rationalized. The doll my father had given me for my first birthday, my constant companion and confidante during the war and throughout my childhood was also a must. Next came the family jewellery —part heirlooms and part items my father had bought at auctions before the war in case we needed to sell something for essentials. The photo albums were declared essential, and I couldn't part with my new burgundy sandals and navy blue suit, the fruit of my first jobs, no matter how unpractical they were. Of course, I couldn't leave behind the new pale blue silk blouse my beloved Great-Aunt Nene had so lovingly created. Three miniature paintings, to sell if the need arose, fitted inside nicely. As we had a little bit more room yet, Mother opened the linen cupboard to look for small pieces of embroidery and lace that might be sellable as well. She couldn't bear to part with the beautiful pink embroidered bedding she had commissioned when she gave birth to me, so we packed it, too. We paraded up and down our apartment, testing the weight of the satchels, and decided we could handle carrying them for hours.

My mother's cousin, Luli, gave us a large sum of cash so we could pay for the "guides" who led people across the border. We packed a net bag with food for a day and we were ready. We met Mariska and her family in the seedy hotel in the early evening. Our mood swung from sadness to nervous laughter and all ranges of emotion in between. We hardly slept on the lumpy beds. At about six in the morning of December 19th, 1956 —before the city awakened— our rag-tag team walked along the wide, empty avenue to the railway station.

For the first couple of hours, the trip to the industrial town of Győr, halfway between the border and Budapest, was uneventful. I stared out the window, wondering if I'd ever see this land again. The new regulations declared you had to have a pass, which of course we didn't have, to travel into the border zone, which was, I think, a hundred kilometres wide, established as an emergency measure by the Hungarian government. So, soon after Győr, our troupe, now swollen to fifteen people, some of them total strangers, had to move into the baggage car to keep out of sight. I was lucky. I had a sled to sit on; probably a gift for some child, but the Christmas tree behind me was prickly. At each station, when the border police came to inspect, all fifteen of us crammed into the single toilet compartment of the car to hide. The largest person sat down on the fixture and the rest of us piled on top of her. This was repeated four or five times until we reached our destination, a small border village, at dusk. We marched to an outlying farmhouse where, packed into the front room, was another small group ready for the crossing.

Suddenly, the door flew open and a very young uniformed border guard burst into the room. "You're all under arrest!" he shouted. "We're shipping you back to Budapest immediately. Anyone attempting to escape will be shot." Silence fell. He left the room and we heard shots ring out in the yard. When he returned, people begged the guard to let them go and plied him with watches, money, and jewellery. He was stony-faced, but accepted the items. He assembled us and we started to march to what we thought surely was prison. There was no sign of our paid "guides." The direction we were going seemed to be wrong to me, but I imagined it could have been the deep dark of the night.

Mother was ready to throw away her satchel as she stumbled from panic and exhaustion among the column of fearful humanity. I grabbed her bag and marched like a robot in silence. I didn't know what to think. Hours later it seemed, although I suspect it was less than half an hour, the guard called us to halt. He pointed into the inky darkness ahead of us and said, "There's the border and I'm going to turn my back on you." It wasn't until a few meters later when Mother tripped on a low wire that I started to believe him. By now, there must have been thirty of us. We marched in silence for an hour across muddy, evenly spaced ruts in the fields that must have been recently ploughed. The mud sucked the shoes off our feet and wrenched our ankles. There was even a blind woman in the group with a seeing-eye dog. The lovely sturdy walking shoes our neighbour had given me for the trip were ruined. The soles separated from the uppers in several places.

I lugged the satchels while looking out for my mother, stumbling along. About an hour into this walk across the fields, an apparition floated ahead of us in the sky. A small town, lit in bluish lights, with a prominent church spire —all the street lights in Hungary were yellow— appeared outlined in mid-air. Our relief was palpable. People broke their self-imposed silence. Ödön remarked we must be close to Budapest by now, because the

170

church spire looked familiar to him. We had been walking for a long time, and it felt as if we had turned around and walked all the way back to Budapest. Everyone laughed at this feeble attempt at humour. The satchels got a little lighter and it seemed the ruts became a little shallower. As we progressed, it became clear the apparition was an Austrian village perched on a plateau. It was the prettiest sight I've ever seen! We marched into the town, finding it hard to temper our happiness and relief at having arrived. All the pent-up tensions of our uncertain day and night bubbled out in noisy, uncontrollable chatter. A few windows opened, begging us to be quieter. The good burghers of the small town of Deutschkreutz had very little sleep for the past month, as groups of Hungarians reached their village each night.

In the centre of the town, we were led to the fire-hall, which was empty save for a thick layer of clean straw topped by a layer of humans of every age, sex, and clad in every kind of garb one could imagine. About three hundred people curled up in the space normally occupied by several fire-trucks. In the foyer, a huge pot of sweet tea with lemon boiled away, and several women volunteers spread jam on slices of bread as fast as their arms could go. Someone begged me to take some, but all I could get down was some of the hot tea. The knot in my stomach was still too tight for me to eat.

I quickly dismissed the thought of bedding down somewhere in a free patch of straw. Our friends arranged for a taxi to go to Vienna, where they had some friends waiting. They had eleven U.S. dollars, just short of what was needed to secure transportation for all of us. Mother and I had no currency. The forints my mother's cousin had given us were spent on the guides; besides, forints were useless anyway, since the cabs accepted only Western money. It was suggested we stay and our friends would get some money in Vienna and send for us. Mother became upset. Never an independent soul, the thought of being left behind alone with me was more than she could handle. An argument ensued, and I couldn't take any more. My facade crumbled and I sat on the spiky wrought iron fence of the church in the Town Square, in the middle of the night, and cried like a three-year-old. My mother stood close by, still arguing with our friends, ignoring my childish outburst. Two young Hungarian men —obviously also new arrivals from across the border— came to ask what the problem was, and I told them. One reached into his pocket and handed my mother two dollar bills to cover the shortfall of the taxi fare for all of us. She tried to repay them with some trinket from our bags, but they just waved her off and disappeared into the night.

In Vienna, we were billeted in a small hotel in the outskirts and it became painfully clear my shoes were ruined. Slush and snow covering the streets kept my feet continually cold and wet. There were several relief agencies set up to help the refugees. For instance, one organization gave everyone a green bag emblazoned with "Unitarian Service Committee" and containing essential hygiene products. Another society gave out large blocks of American processed cheese and powdered milk. We had cheese and reconstituted milk warmed on the hotel room radiator for supper for a month. Depots of used clothing were set up all over the city. The refugees gave tips to each other about where to get things. After several unsuccessful attempts, I finally landed a good pair of emerald-green leather shoes that fit well, although they didn't go with anything I wore. It didn't matter. All the refugees were clad in similarly mismatched attire. At this point, nobody cared, as long as they were warm and safe. The refugees walked the streets for hours, admiring the well-stocked shop windows. Mother and I often bumped into friends and acquaintances. We exchanged news about mutual friends and about where each one was heading to in this exodus.

Mother got in touch with her brother in Spain, but he discouraged us from trying to go there. Women couldn't make a living, and he wasn't doing well enough to consider taking responsibility for us. He suggested we try to go to Canada or the U.S. He sent us a little money to supplement the handouts. The larger problem was for us to get a visa for one of those countries.

The U.S. quota for refugees was closed. Only sponsored immigrants were considered. We didn't have a sponsor. The same situation faced us at the Canadian Embassy, where a small crowd of refugees milled around in the square in front of the building.

Up to early December, the Embassy had handed out nameless appointments on slips of paper for processing into Canada to all who asked. But if people succeeded in getting into the U.S., or decided to wait for other family members, they didn't need those slips and gave them to others who needed them. We wandered about the square for about half an hour until we found a man who had an extra slip. After a cursory medical exam, we were told to show up at the railroad station in a few days to be transported to the Canadian refugee camp in Wiener Neustadt where we would be gathered, processed and assigned transportation to Canada.

The Canadian camp at Wiener Neustadt was rumoured to be a former Nazi concentration camp. Some of the kids who arrived earlier took the newcomers to the ruins they claimed were the crematorium. I never tracked down whether this story was true. With nothing to do, the camp was always rife with rumours. The place certainly wasn't pleasant. The barrack-like structure had unheated bathrooms with rows of twenty sinks and toilets. It was so cold that water had frozen in most of the sinks. We were assigned cots in the middle room of a group of three, each containing metal beds with straw mattresses for ten to twelve people. Children, adults, couples, singles, strangers and families were all heaped together. There was a pot-bellied stove in one corner, valiantly trying to emit some comfort. Those near the stove roasted, while those in the next row froze. The windows leaked so badly, we put extra straw mattresses against them to try to keep out the cold. Luckily, we only stayed three days. Nevertheless, the food, although basic, was plentiful, hot, and we enjoyed the luxury of having meat daily. The mess hall, well heated, doubled as a classroom for English lessons between meals. I attended as many classes as offered in preparation for our new life in Canada.

At dawn on January 23rd, we were bussed to the train that was to take us to the port city of Bremenhaven in Germany to sail for Canada. One picture is engraved in my memory. I shivered in the early dawn, waiting for the bus, when I saw in the well-lit doorway of the barracks the outline of a figure holding a fencing sword in one hand and a helmet tucked under the other arm. The picture was so incongruous that I stifled a giggle. I later found out he was a young fencing champion, holding the items he treasured most. The train trip took all day and the next night. As we neared Bremenhaven, Mother could hardly contain herself. Her brother, whom she hadn't seen for twenty years, had promised to try to meet us at the ship. I was looking forward to seeing my larger-than-life uncle for the first time. As the train slowly pulled into the station, grey with drizzle, there was no one to be seen. Then, suddenly, a lone figure came into view. Mother shrieked, and I knew it must be my Uncle Róbert.

He accompanied us onto the ship, bought me a Coke --my very first-- in the bar and gave us warm scarves and a big box of dates and figs for snacking on the voyage. The visit was over in a couple of hours, and we sailed for Canada. Almost as soon as we passed the marvellous white cliffs of Dover, the sea turned mean and we spent most of our time being seasick. Whenever possible, we made it to the after-dinner dance, which was great fun. There were a number of young German and Yugoslavian immigrants aboard, in addition to our group of Hungarian refugees, meaning plenty of dance partners, even for a fifteen-year-old. The immigrants were dressed in their most elegant duds, while the refugees sported the mismatched hand-me-downs they had collected from the relief agencies.

We arrived in Halifax on the afternoon of February fourth. The day was overcast and drizzly as we crowded the decks to get our first glimpse of Canada. We spent the night on the ship in harbour and in the morning, we were led to a great hall for processing and from there onto our train for Winnipeg. Since most of the refugees knew little or nothing about Canada, had they been given a choice, they would have wanted to go to Montreal or Toronto, the only two places they had heard about from former immigrants. It would have been hard for those cities to provide such a large number of newcomers with jobs and temporary accommodations. Immigration decided to send each boatload or planeload to a different Canadian city to even out the burden.

The train was fabulous. We had never seen anything like it.

It sported luxurious plush seats, friendly black porters in crisp uniforms, shiny brass fittings, polished wood everywhere, and boxes of Kellogg's Cornflakes in every nook and cranny. We had never seen cornflakes before, and never had dry cereal for breakfast. After tasting it, we decided it was the Canadian equivalent of potato chips and snacked on it dry during the whole trip. As we left Halifax, we saw an occasional house here or there, but the sparseness of the population was odd to us mostly city folks. Even odder were the bright pastel colours of the houses. As the wheels clicked away the miles, day and night, with plenty of time to think and talk, a few people had panic attacks now that we were nearing our unfamiliar destination. The enormity of what had happened to us in the last few months, and the scary prospect of having to start a new life in a strange land and having to speak a language few of the refugees knew, struck the weak. The stronger ones continued to plot and plan to conquer adversity, and soar to great success now that they were truly free. Others relieved their tension with jokes and wisecracks, to the merriment of the group. I often wonder how a psychologist would have evaluated the mood swings of our little troupe.

In Montreal, a few of our sponsored compatriots, as well as a few adventurous ones, decided to stay behind, even though they were told there would be no help in getting settled from the Immigration Department if they didn't continue to our assigned destination, Winnipeg. From Montreal to Winnipeg, crossing the Canadian Shield, we hardly saw any populated areas. The sun shone brightly as frozen lakes followed forests and vice versa.

On February 8th, we arrived in Winnipeg. On the platform, a contingent of middle-aged ladies wearing silk dresses, straw hats, and fur jackets waited to welcome us, to minister to us and help ease our way into becoming Canadian. Our ragtag group, emerging from the train, suppressed a collective giggle at their elegance that clashed with our own dilapidated clothes. Nevertheless, the intentions of the ladies soon proved to be genuine, even if their understanding of our plight was somewhat deficient. The ladies spoke no Hungarian, and we spoke no English. We communicated with hands and smiles.

With their kind help and that of countless others, we started our long and often arduous trek into becoming Canadians.

Being a refugee is like being an adopted child, with all the ambivalent feelings and loyalties. Love for the birth parent or in this case the homeland is embedded like the genes of an adopted child, but the loyalty for the adoptive country, born from gratitude, is usually so strong as to always cause conflict within the refugee's heart. For instance, one favourite question among refugee groups is, "Who do you root for during the Olympics?" which usually elicits a lively debate that clearly shows the confusion of divided loyalties refugees feel.

For example, in hockey, I root for Canada. I learned to love this sport here from my second stepfather. My loyalty is definitely with the Canadian team when it comes to swimming, because I was an official of the Canadian Amateur Swimming Association when my son was a competitive swimmer, and back then I personally knew all the swimmers. However, I will root for the Hungarian competitor if no Canadian is entered in the event, because I remember the impromptu parade in my neighbourhood in 1952 when the champion swimmers where carried home on the crowd's shoulders. The various skiing events cause no problem. Living in the Rocky Mountains, my skiing loyalty definitely belongs to Canada, or more specifically to the Bow Valley athletes. In other events, I choose the individual or team from my two homelands that seems to be more accomplished in the particular sport. Luckily, there hasn't been an instance when a Hungarian athlete was competing head-to-head against a Canadian at any Olympics. I would have been in big trouble then!

There is a subtle and often blurry difference between immigrants and refugees. An immigrant has consciously planned to leave his or her home and settle in a different country. There was time to choose, read up and familiarize oneself with the country, its culture and language. The refugees, on the other hand, were uprooted suddenly and thrust into a strange land, usually following some dramatic, stressful events in their birth-land. Each refugee has a story to tell about his or her path to and arrival in Canada. The details may differ, but the message is usually the same.

The majority of refugees are the greatest flag-waving patriots in Canada. We came to this country in the wake of turmoil and danger in our homeland; penniless, destitute, still in mourning and in shock of having lost our home, friends and relatives in the span of a few turbulent weeks. We were confused, scared of our future, and found our dignity in tatters. We arrived in Canada to find caring people, helping hands and a warm welcome. Through the years, we tried to achieve the success we dreamed of, succeeding at times and failing at others, but we knew this great country, Canada, gave us the freedom to try again, in any way we desired. Here, we could keep our culture and pride of ethnic origin, yet become Canadian and raise our family in guarantied peace. Show me another country that provides all that and asks nothing in return for its hospitality.

If you see a former refugee stand a little taller or have shiny eyes during the singing of "O Canada," don't be surprised. That's our way of saying, "Thank you, Canada! We love you!"

———

I recently donated one of the bags we carried, the pink bedding, a photo of my doll, and the ship's passenger list to Pier 21 Exhibition Hall in Halifax, dedicated to immigrants and refugees who were processed into Canada through the Pier 21 immigration facilities. Mother kept her stocking repair machine for decades in the back of her closet —unused. She got rid of it sometime in the 1980's, but kept the needles that went with it. I have those now as a memento of the past.

Because the memories of those days were too painful, it's only recently, fifty years after the fact, that I could face them and write about them. Previously, if asked about my experiences, I answered as briefly as possible, closing the door on the memories as quickly as good manners allowed. I never tracked down what our camp was originally. I was afraid of the answers. Just recently, I found out, thanks to the extensive research conducted by Mr. Maurice Servranckx, that it's highly unlikely the rumours were true. There were several German factories in the area using prisoners as forced labourers from the concentration camp of Mauthausen, but there were no extermination camps in Wiener Neustadt. More recent private communications from a former inmate indicate that there indeed was a forced-labour camp in Wiener Neustadt, but it was a bombed out factory. Perhaps those were the ruins the children showed us. Judging by the rows of toilets and sinks, I would guess the brick buildings we were housed in were formerly used as an army barracks, as a hospital, or possibly a residential school. Badly damaged during the war, the buildings were never repaired before being pressed into emergency service to organize the collection of refugees bound for Canada. Because our stay was short, a matter of three or four days, none of the refugees ever resented this inconvenience.

I became something of a hero on that trip. My geography teacher was an exceptional lady who poured huge quantities of information into our reluctant heads. As a result, I knew a little about Winnipeg and could cite some of the information learned about industry, transportation and agriculture. I also managed to have a vocabulary of twenty words of English, so I was used as an "interpreter" to communicate with the porters.

The long trip, and having to face the same problems together, built a special relationship among the people who shared this trek into the unknown. We became a very special "family," in which we could understand each other's emotions. For instance, later, the young fencer and I were the only two Hungarian refugees, in different faculties, among seven thousand students at the University of Manitoba. We relied heavily on that mutual support during our first two years.

Appendix

Historical Background

I was very hesitant to write this chapter on the history of Hungary in the twentieth century, for several reasons. In school, the teachers followed the strict communist doctrine, often leaving significant chunks out or giving a skewed version, for fear of touching something controversial or because the curriculum demanded it. While my grandmother, and to a lesser extent my mother, told me of the "olden days," their scope was limited to their immediate surroundings. Neither of them were interested in politics. My stepfather, Zoli, though politically inclined, sheltered me from such a complex subject, partly because he felt I was too young, partly because if I repeated his views outside our home, he could get into serious trouble. My understanding came from snippets of conversation caught here and there, when the adults didn't think I was listening and to a great extent, from the satirical caricature magazine, Ludas Matyi, that I bought weekly. Hardly qualifications to write authoritatively on the subject!

It's only in recent years that I began to study Hungary's history in the twentieth century. I've learned that each regime and each political entity, even today, have put their own spin on the events to such an extent that it's hard to separate the truth from the interpretation and misinformation. Nevertheless, I will attempt to give a brief outline of the major events that played a part in my story.

At the end of the nineteenth and the beginning of the twentieth century, Hungary was a progressive, flourishing member of the Austro-Hungarian Monarchy. Buda, Óbuda and Pest joined to form Budapest in 1873. Buda, on the west bank of the Danube, was the historical royal seat of power. Óbuda, to the north, was home to many craftsmen and some industrial activity. Pest, on the east bank, was the city of business with its shops, transportation lines and industry, a fertile ground for trade and commerce. Major building activity followed the unification of the three cities, producing many architectural masterpieces in anticipation of the celebration of Hungary's millennium of the Magyar conquest of the Carpathian Basin. Millennial festivities were celebrated with great pomp, and an exposition in 1896 attracted dignitaries from all over the world. Budapest was alive and sparkling with intellectuals, artists and artisans.

The Austro-Hungarian Monarchy entered the First World War as an ally of Germany. The long-drawn out war and the defeat resulted in the collapse of the multi-national monarchy. After the break-up, Hungary regained its complete independence, became a republic under Mihály Károlyi, whose position became untenable as a result of repeated military incursions and occupation of Hungarian territories by the neighbouring countries. He handed over power to the social democrats that formed a coalition government with the communists under Béla Kun, a former POW in Russia. After 133 days of wild social experimentation, the Hungarian Soviet Republic was overthrown by troops from Romania, occupying a major part of Hungary and spending several weeks camped in Budapest. They supported the counterrevolutionary government of Admiral Miklós Horthy. The Romanians withdrew from Budapest and later, from the rest of eastern Hungary as the counterrevolutionaries and a national army gathering in French-occupied Szeged in southern Hungary moved north. In November 1919, they entered Budapest. The leader of this army was Miklós Horthy, admiral of the Austro-Hungarian navy. All this happened in little more than a year. In the meantime, the Treaty of Trianon was formulated by the Allies, which in 1920 stripped Hungary of two-thirds of its land and more than half of its population. Admiral Horthy became regent in the new independent kingdom that had no king. Politically, the country enjoyed relative stability. By the second half of the 1920s, Hungary more or less managed to solve the economic problems brought about by the lost war and the loss of its territories. However, the worldwide depression affected businesses in the

1930s.

In the late 1920s, the Hungarian government made overtures to Italy and later to Germany. The two countries were very much dissatisfied with the status quo and promised Hungary a revision of the Versailles treaties. The shift to the political right resulted in passing laws curtailing the rights of the economically and culturally important Jewish Hungarians. Hungary was drawn to fascist Germany and Italy with promises to restore the territories lost at Trianon. The country entered the Second World War on June 26, 1941, by declaring war on the Soviet Union and the United States. The ensuing battles on the Russian front almost completely destroyed the ill-equipped army. On March 19, 1944, Germany, not trusting Hungary's loyalty to the Nazi cause, occupied the country. Realizing the war was lost, Admiral Horthy announced his country's withdrawal from the war on October 15th of the same year. Before he could act, the Arrow Cross Party–the Hungarian equivalent of the Nazi party–backed by the Germans and led by Ferenc Szálasi seized power from Horthy. Hungary remained an ally of Germany to the bitter end. The Soviet Army was heading west and on December 21, 1944, established the Provisional Government in Debrecen, the most easterly major city in Hungary. In January 1945, the Soviet Army reached Budapest, but the fierce resistance of the retreating German Army necessitated a long house-to-house battle to free the city, resulting in loss of many civilian lives, the destruction of many buildings, all of the Danube bridges and much of the infrastructure. The citizens of Budapest were particularly stunned when the Germans blew up their beautiful bridges as they withdrew to the west. The Germans, with some Hungarian military help, continued their fight for some time, particularly in the Castle Hill district, where underground passages gave them effective cover. The devastation of this historic area defies description.

In 1947, the Communist Party got more votes than any other party did, but at twenty-two percent, it was far from a majority. However, soon after with complex political manipulations, they took over the government from the coalition and the era ruled by Mátyas Rákosi began. The following year

182

nationalizations, the expropriation of land, factories and businesses without compensation, began. The forced collectivization of farms reduced the agricultural output, resulting in food shortages, while the factories, lacking raw materials and replacement parts, weren't producing enough goods to satisfy the needs of the population. To make matters worse, the centralized distribution system was inefficient in delivering material to where it was needed. Show trials, expunging the real and imagined enemies of the state, were staged to keep the discontented population under control.

On October 23, 1956, university students demonstrated, demanding the withdrawal of the Soviet troops stationed in Hungary. Within hours, the peaceful march became a revolution when the Hungarian secret police fired upon demonstrators at the National Radio. The next day, Imre Nagy, a prominent moderate communist figure, was declared Prime Minister. Heavy street battles took place in sections of the city between the rebels and the secret police, with some units of the army backing each side. Radio Free Europe encouraged the fight, announcing that U.S. help was on its way. At first the Russians withdrew, but they returned and on November 4th, laid siege to the city of Budapest. Russian tanks rumbled down the elegant boulevard and once again, the city was in ruins. Although the fighting continued for another week, the revolution was lost. Three thousand were killed, and two hundred thousand people headed to Austria in search of freedom.

Internet Bibliography
– for readers who wish to get further information about Hungary

Wikipedia on Hungary
– an extensive site with many links
http://en.wikipedia.org/wiki/Hungary

Hungarian Government Website –
http://www.magyarorszag.hu/angol

Portals to the World – Hungary
http://www.loc.gov/rr/international/european/hungary/hu.html

The Institute for the History of the 1956 Hungarian Revolution
http://www.rev.hu/index_en.html

Corvinus Library – Hungarian History
http://www.hungarian-history.hu

Videofact International Documentary Press
– The Hungarian Revolution
http://www.videofact.com/english/more7.htm

The Secret Police, AVO
http://www.globalsecurity.org/intell/world/hungary/avh.htm

History and Pictures of Budapest
http://www.fsz.bme.hu/hungary/budapest/budapest.htm

The Hungarian Tourist Office – Pictures and information
http://www.hungary.com/

Statue Park
http://www.szoborpark.hu/en/en_index.php

Pictures of Budapest
http://www.mozgomedia.com/budapest/opener.htm

Visit Budapest on this Tourist Information Page
http://www.budapestinfo.hu/en/

Acknowledgements:

This book wouldn't have been possible without the help of a number of individuals and their contributions are gratefully acknowledged:

M.D. Benoit (mdbenoit.com), author of the science fiction novel "Metered Space," for editing and critiques

Peter Ungar for advice on typography, cover art, layout and enthusiastic support

Robert Weisz for wading through the first draft and pronouncing it worthy of publication and his encouragement of during this project

Eva S. Balogh Ph. D. (Yale) without whose willingness to correct the Historical Background chapter I have dared to touch that subject.

Elizabeth Delisi, (www.elizabethdelisi.com), author and editor for correcting the final copy.

The author is also indebted to her husband, son, daughter-in-law, family and friends for their encouragement, support and help given in her efforts to remember.

Try Kay Enterprises
P.O. Box 8084
Canmore, AB.
T1W 2T8
Canada
www.telusplanet.net/public/ekende
Phone/fax: 403-678-5821